Crochet Fashionista

Elevate Your Style with Innovative Crochet Techniques in This Book

Alexander R Darryl

THIS BOOK

BELONGS TO

....

Thank you for Purchasing my book and taking the time to read it from front to back. I am always grateful when a reader chooses my work and I hope you enjoyed it!

With the vast selection available online, I am touched that you chose to be purchasing my work and take valuable time out of your life to read it. My hope is that you feel you made the right decision.

I very much would like to know what you thought of the book. Please take the time to write an honest and informative review on Amazon.com. Your experience and opinions will be of great benefit to me and those readers looking to make an informed choice.

With much thanks.

Table of Contents

SUMMARY

Introduction to Crochet Hacking: Unleashing Your Creativity and Innovation in Crochet

Crochet hacking, also known as "crochet hacking" or "crochet innovation," is a fascinating and exciting approach to the traditional craft of crochet. It involves taking the basic techniques and stitches of crochet and pushing the boundaries to create unique and innovative designs. Crochet hacking allows crocheters to unleash their creativity and explore new possibilities in the world of crochet.

In traditional crochet, crocheters follow patterns and instructions to create specific items such as blankets, scarves, or hats. While this is a great way to learn and practice crochet, crochet hacking takes it a step further by encouraging crocheters to think outside the box and experiment with different techniques, stitches, and materials.

One of the key aspects of crochet hacking is the idea of customization. Instead of following a set pattern, crocheters can modify and adapt existing patterns to suit their own preferences and style. This could involve changing the stitch pattern, altering the size or shape of the item, or adding unique embellishments. Crochet hacking allows crocheters to truly make a piece their own and express their individuality through their creations.

Another aspect of crochet hacking is the use of unconventional materials. While traditional crochet typically uses yarn, crochet hackers often incorporate other materials such as fabric, ribbon, wire, or even recycled materials into their projects. This opens up a whole new world of possibilities and allows for the creation of truly one-of-a-kind pieces.

Crochet hacking also encourages crocheters to experiment with different techniques and stitches. By combining different stitches or using them in unconventional ways, crocheters can create interesting textures and patterns that are not typically seen in traditional crochet. This adds depth and dimension to their projects and allows for endless creativity.

In addition to customization and experimentation, crochet hacking also promotes problem-solving and innovation. When faced with a challenge or a design problem, crochet hackers find creative solutions and think outside the box to overcome obstacles. This problem-solving mindset not only enhances their crochet skills but also fosters a sense of accomplishment and satisfaction.

Crochet hacking is not just about creating unique and innovative designs; it is also about fostering a sense of community and sharing knowledge. Crochet hackers often come together in online forums, social media groups, or local meetups to share their ideas, techniques, and projects. This sense of community allows for collaboration, inspiration, and support among fellow crochet hackers.

The Rise of Sustainable Fashion Through Crochet: In recent years, there has been a significant rise in the popularity of sustainable fashion, with consumers becoming more conscious of the environmental and social impact of their clothing choices. One particular trend that has gained traction in the sustainable fashion movement is crochet.

Crochet, a technique of creating fabric by interlocking loops of yarn or thread using a crochet hook, has been around for centuries.

However, it has recently experienced a resurgence in popularity as a sustainable fashion choice. This is due to several reasons.

Firstly, crochet is a highly versatile and adaptable craft. It can be used to create a wide range of garments and accessories, from sweaters and dresses to hats and bags. This versatility allows designers to experiment with different styles and designs, catering to a diverse range of fashion tastes. Additionally, crochet can be easily customized and tailored to fit individual body shapes and sizes, promoting a more inclusive and body-positive approach to fashion.

Secondly, crochet is a sustainable and eco-friendly alternative to mass-produced clothing. The process of crocheting involves using yarn or thread made from natural fibers, such as cotton, hemp, or bamboo. These fibers are biodegradable and renewable, unlike synthetic materials like polyester or nylon, which contribute to the growing problem of textile waste. By choosing crochet garments, consumers can reduce their carbon footprint and support a more sustainable fashion industry.

Furthermore, crochet is a craft that encourages creativity and craftsmanship. Unlike fast fashion, which prioritizes speed and quantity, crochet requires time, patience, and skill. Each crochet piece is handmade, often with intricate patterns and stitches, showcasing the artistry and dedication of the maker. This emphasis on craftsmanship promotes a more mindful and appreciative approach to fashion, encouraging consumers to value quality over quantity.

In addition to its environmental benefits, crochet also has social implications. The rise of sustainable fashion through crochet has created opportunities for marginalized communities and artisans around the world. Many crochet garments are produced by independent designers or small-scale cooperatives, providing fair wages and empowering individuals in developing countries. By supporting crochet fashion, consumers can contribute to the economic empowerment of these communities and promote social justice within the fashion industry.

Overall, the rise of sustainable fashion through crochet represents a shift towards a more conscious and responsible approach to clothing. By choosing crochet garments, consumers can support a more sustainable and ethical fashion industry, while also embracing creativity, craftsmanship, and individuality.

Defining Crochet Hacking: A Marriage of Mending and Creativity: Crochet hacking can be defined as the innovative combination of mending and creativity within the realm of crochet. It involves using crochet techniques and skills to repair or enhance various items, such as clothing, accessories, or even household items. This unique approach to crochet not only serves the purpose of fixing or restoring items, but also adds a touch of personalization and creativity to them.

One of the key aspects of crochet hacking is the utilization of crochet stitches and techniques to mend or reinforce damaged or worn-out items. For example, if a sweater has a hole or a tear, instead of simply patching it up with a plain piece of fabric, crochet hacking involves using crochet stitches to create a decorative and functional repair. This can be done by crocheting over the damaged area, creating a unique and visually appealing design that not only fixes the issue but also adds a new element to the garment.

In addition to mending, crochet hacking also involves the creative aspect of crochet. It allows individuals to explore their imagination and come up with innovative ways to incorporate crochet into various items. This can include adding crochet embellishments to clothing, such as crocheted flowers or appliques, or even creating entirely new items by combining crochet with other materials, such as fabric or leather.

Crochet hacking is not limited to clothing and accessories; it can also be applied to household items. For example, instead of throwing away a worn-out cushion cover, crochet hacking allows individuals to breathe new life into it by adding crochet details or even creating a completely new cover using crochet techniques. This not only saves money and reduces waste but also adds a unique and personalized touch to the home decor.

Furthermore, crochet hacking encourages sustainability and eco-consciousness. By repairing and repurposing items through crochet, individuals can reduce their consumption and contribute to a more sustainable lifestyle. It promotes the idea of making the most out of what we already have, rather than constantly buying new items.

Overall, crochet hacking is a marriage of mending and creativity within the world of crochet. It combines the practicality of fixing and restoring items with the artistic expression of crochet. It allows individuals to not only mend and enhance their belongings but also to add a personal touch and unleash their creativity. With its focus on sustainability and innovation, crochet hacking is a versatile and exciting approach to crochet that opens up endless possibilities for individuals to explore and create.

The History and Cultural Significance of Mending Clothes by Crochet: Mending clothes by crochet has a rich history and holds significant cultural importance. Crochet, a technique of creating fabric using a hooked needle, has been used for centuries to repair and mend garments. This method of mending not only extends the lifespan of clothing but also adds a unique and artistic touch to the repaired piece.

The history of mending clothes by crochet can be traced back to ancient times. In many cultures, crochet was used as a practical skill to mend and reinforce clothing. The technique was particularly popular in rural communities where resources were scarce, and people had to make the most out of what they had. Crochet allowed individuals to repair their garments without the need for expensive materials or specialized tools.

Over time, mending clothes by crochet evolved from a purely practical necessity to a form of creative expression. As the technique became more refined, artisans began to incorporate intricate patterns and designs into their mending work. This added a decorative element to the repaired clothing, transforming it into a unique piece of art.

In addition to its practical and artistic value, mending clothes by crochet also holds cultural significance. In many societies, the act of mending clothes is seen as a symbol of resourcefulness, frugality, and sustainability. It reflects a mindset of valuing and preserving what one already has, rather than constantly seeking new and disposable items. Mending clothes by crochet embodies the idea of making do with what is available and finding beauty in imperfection.

Furthermore, mending clothes by crochet can also be seen as a way to connect with one's heritage and cultural roots. Many traditional patterns and techniques have been passed down through generations, preserving the knowledge and skills of previous artisans. By continuing to mend clothes using crochet, individuals can honor their cultural heritage and keep these traditions alive.

In recent years, there has been a resurgence of interest in mending clothes by crochet. As the world becomes more aware of the environmental impact of fast fashion and the importance of sustainable practices, people are turning to traditional techniques like crochet to repair and repurpose their clothing. This renewed interest not only helps reduce waste but also fosters a sense of creativity and individuality in fashion.

In conclusion, mending clothes by crochet has a long and storied history, rooted in practicality, creativity, and cultural significance. This technique not only extends the lifespan of garments but also adds a unique and artistic touch to the repaired piece.

Environmental Impact and the Benefits of Upcycling in Repairing Clothes with Crochet

In recent years, there has been a growing concern about the environmental impact of the fashion industry. The production and disposal of clothing contribute to pollution, waste, and the depletion of natural resources. As a result, many individuals and organizations are seeking sustainable alternatives to reduce the negative effects of fashion on the environment. One such alternative is upcycling, a process that involves transforming old or discarded materials into new and useful products. When it comes to repairing clothes, upcycling with crochet has emerged as a popular and effective method.

The environmental impact of the fashion industry is significant. The production of clothing involves the use of vast amounts of water, energy, and chemicals. Additionally, the disposal of clothing contributes to the growing problem of textile waste. According to the Environmental Protection Agency (EPA), in 2018 alone, over 17 million tons of textile waste were generated in the United States, with only 15.2% being recycled. This waste ends up in landfills, where it takes years to decompose and releases harmful greenhouse gases into the atmosphere.

Upcycling with crochet offers a sustainable solution to this problem. By repairing clothes using crochet techniques, individuals can extend the lifespan of their garments and reduce the need for new clothing purchases. Crochet involves using a hook to create interlocking loops of yarn, thread, or other materials, resulting in a durable and visually appealing fabric. This technique can be used to mend holes, reinforce weak areas, or add decorative elements to clothing, making it both functional and aesthetically pleasing.

One of the key benefits of upcycling with crochet is the reduction of textile waste. By repairing clothes instead of discarding them, individuals can prevent perfectly usable garments from ending up in landfills. This not only reduces the demand for new clothing production but also saves valuable resources such as water and energy. Additionally, upcycling with crochet allows for the customization and personalization of clothing, giving old garments a new lease on life and reducing the desire for fast fashion trends.

Furthermore, upcycling with crochet promotes a more sustainable and ethical approach to fashion. By repairing and reusing clothing, individuals can reduce their carbon footprint and contribute to a circular economy. The circular economy aims to minimize waste and maximize the value of resources by keeping products and materials in use for as long as possible.

Crochet Tools and Materials for Hacking by Crochet: Crochet Tools and Materials for Hacking by Crochet is a comprehensive guide that provides detailed information on the essential tools and materials needed for successful crochet projects. Whether you are a beginner or an experienced crocheter, this guide will help you understand the importance of using the right tools and materials to achieve the desired results.

One of the most important tools for crochet is the crochet hook. This tool comes in various sizes and materials, such as aluminum, steel, or plastic. The size of the crochet hook determines the size of the stitches, so it is crucial to choose the right size for your project. Additionally, the material of the crochet hook can affect the tension and drape of the finished piece, so it is important to consider your personal preferences and the desired outcome when selecting a crochet hook.

Another essential tool for crochet is a pair of scissors. While it may seem like a basic tool, having a good pair of scissors specifically designed for cutting yarn can make a significant difference in the ease and precision of your crochet work. Yarn can be thick and difficult to cut with regular scissors, so investing in a pair of sharp, durable scissors will save you time and frustration.

In addition to crochet hooks and scissors, there are several other tools that can enhance your crochet experience. Stitch markers are small, removable markers that can be placed on your work to mark specific stitches or sections. These markers are especially useful when working on complex patterns or when you need to keep track of stitch counts. Tapestry needles are another essential tool for crochet, as they are used to weave in loose ends and sew pieces together. These needles have a large eye and a blunt tip, making them easy to thread and maneuver through stitches.

When it comes to materials, the type and quality of yarn you choose can greatly impact the outcome of your crochet project. Yarn comes in various fibers, weights, and textures, each with its own unique characteristics. For beginners, it is recommended to start with a medium-weight yarn made of acrylic or a blend of acrylic and wool. These types of yarn are affordable, easy to work with, and come in a wide range of colors. As you gain more experience, you can explore different fibers such as cotton, silk, or alpaca, which offer different textures and drape.

Furthermore, the color and pattern of the yarn can also play a significant role in the overall look of your crochet project.

Fundamental Crochet Stitches and Techniques for Repair Clothes with Crochet: In this guide, we will explore the fundamental crochet stitches and techniques that can be used to repair clothes using crochet. Crochet is a versatile craft that can be used to mend and enhance garments, giving them a new lease of life.

Firstly, let's delve into the basic crochet stitches that are essential for repairing clothes. The chain stitch is the foundation of crochet and is used to create a base for your work. It is created by making a slipknot and then pulling the yarn through the loop, repeating this process until you have the desired number of chains. The single crochet stitch is another important stitch, as it is used to create a tight and sturdy fabric. It involves inserting the hook into the stitch, pulling the yarn through, and then pulling the yarn through both loops on the hook. The double crochet stitch is slightly taller than the single crochet and is created by yarn over, inserting the hook into the stitch, pulling the yarn through, yarn over again, and pulling through two loops at a time until you have one loop left on the hook.

Now that we have covered the basic stitches, let's move on to the techniques that can be used to repair clothes with crochet. One common technique is to use crochet to mend holes or tears in fabric. To do this, you can create a patch using crochet and then sew it onto the garment. This not only repairs the damage but also adds a unique and decorative touch to the clothing. Another technique is to add crochet embellishments to garments that may have worn-out areas. For example, you can crochet flowers, leaves, or other motifs and then sew them onto the garment to cover up any imperfections.

In addition to repairing clothes, crochet can also be used to enhance and personalize garments. You can add crochet edgings to hems, cuffs, or collars to give them a delicate and feminine touch. This can be done using simple stitches such as the single crochet or more intricate stitches like the shell stitch. Crochet can also be used to create decorative appliques that can be sewn onto clothing, adding a unique and individualized flair.

When repairing clothes with crochet, it is important to choose the right yarn and hook size for the project. For mending small holes or tears, a fine yarn and a small hook size are recommended. However, if you are adding crochet embellishments or edgings, you may want to use a thicker yarn and a larger hook size to create a more substantial and noticeable effect.

Understanding Fabric and Yarn Compatibility of Repair Clothes with Crochet: When it comes to repairing clothes with crochet, it is essential to have a good understanding of fabric and yarn compatibility. This knowledge will not only ensure that your repairs are effective and long-lasting but also prevent any further damage to the garment.

Firstly, let's discuss fabric compatibility. Different fabrics have different properties, such as stretch, weight, and texture. It is important to choose a yarn that complements the fabric you are working with. For example, if you are repairing a stretchy knit fabric, you would want to use a yarn that has some elasticity to it, such as a blend of acrylic and nylon. This will allow your repair to stretch and move with the fabric, preventing any strain on the repaired area.

Similarly, the weight of the yarn should match the weight of the fabric. If you are repairing a lightweight, delicate fabric, using a bulky yarn may cause the repair to look bulky and out of place. On the other hand, using a thin, lightweight yarn on a heavy fabric may not provide enough support and durability. It is important to find a balance between the yarn weight and the fabric weight to ensure a seamless repair.

Texture is another factor to consider when choosing yarn for repairing clothes. If the fabric has a smooth texture, using a yarn with a similar smooth texture will help the repair blend in seamlessly. However, if the fabric has a textured or ribbed surface, using a yarn with a contrasting texture, such as a boucle or a twisted yarn, can create an interesting visual effect.

In addition to fabric compatibility, it is also crucial to consider the compatibility of the yarn with the existing stitches in the garment. If the garment was originally crocheted, it is best to use the same type of yarn and stitch pattern for the repair. This will ensure that the repair seamlessly integrates with the existing stitches and maintains the overall aesthetic of the garment.

If the garment was not originally crocheted, it is important to choose a yarn and stitch pattern that closely matches the existing fabric. This will help the repair blend in and appear as if it was part of the original design. Taking the time to carefully select the right yarn and stitch pattern will result in a repair that is not only functional but also visually appealing.

In conclusion, understanding fabric and yarn compatibility is crucial when repairing clothes with crochet. By considering factors such as fabric properties, yarn weight, texture, and existing stitches, you can ensure that your repairs are effective, durable, and aesthetically pleasing.

Assessing Your Clothes: Deciding What to Mend and Refashion in Repair Clothes with Crochet: When it comes to assessing your clothes and deciding what to mend and refashion, Repair Clothes with Crochet is here to guide you through the process. This comprehensive guide will help you make informed decisions about which items in your wardrobe are worth repairing and transforming using crochet techniques.

Firstly, it is important to evaluate the condition of your clothes. Look for signs of wear and tear such as holes, loose threads, or missing buttons. Assess the overall quality of the fabric and determine if it is worth investing time and effort into repairing. Some garments may be beyond repair, especially if the fabric is severely damaged or if the cost of repair outweighs the value of the item.

Once you have identified the pieces that are worth mending, Repair Clothes with Crochet provides step-by-step instructions on how to mend them using crochet techniques. Crochet is a versatile craft that can be used to repair various types of damage, from small holes to larger tears. The book offers detailed explanations and illustrations to help you master the necessary crochet stitches and techniques.

In addition to mending, Repair Clothes with Crochet also explores the art of refashioning. This involves transforming your clothes into something new and unique using crochet. The book provides creative ideas and inspiration for refashioning different types of garments, such as turning a plain t-shirt into a trendy crochet top or adding crochet embellishments to a plain dress.

The benefits of repairing and refashioning your clothes with crochet are numerous. Not only does it save you money by extending the lifespan of your garments, but it also allows you to express your creativity and personal style. By repairing and refashioning your clothes, you are reducing waste and contributing to a more sustainable fashion industry.

Repair Clothes with Crochet goes beyond just providing instructions. It also offers tips and tricks for selecting the right yarn and crochet hooks for your projects, as well as advice on how to care for your repaired and refashioned garments to ensure their longevity.

Whether you are a beginner or an experienced crocheter, Repair Clothes with Crochet is a valuable resource that will empower you to take control of your wardrobe. With its detailed instructions, creative ideas, and practical tips, this book will inspire you to mend and refashion your clothes using crochet techniques, creating a wardrobe that is both stylish and sustainable.

Deconstructing Garments for Upcycling in Repair Clothes with Crochet: Deconstructing garments for upcycling in repair clothes with crochet is a creative and sustainable approach to extending the lifespan of clothing items. This process involves taking apart old or damaged garments and repurposing the fabric and materials to create new and unique pieces using crochet techniques.

The first step in this process is to carefully deconstruct the garment. This involves removing any buttons, zippers, or other fasteners, as well as any linings or interfacing. The main fabric of the garment is then carefully cut into smaller pieces, taking care to preserve as much usable fabric as possible. This deconstruction process requires patience and attention to detail, as it is important to avoid damaging the fabric or materials during this step.

Once the garment has been deconstructed, the next step is to assess the fabric and materials for their potential use in crochet projects. This can include examining the fabric for any stains, tears, or other imperfections that may need to be worked around or repaired. It is also important to consider the weight, texture, and drape of the fabric, as these factors will influence the types of crochet projects that can be created.

After assessing the fabric, the next step is to decide on the crochet projects that will be created using the upcycled materials. This can range from simple repairs, such as patching holes or reinforcing seams, to more complex projects, such as creating new garments or accessories. The possibilities are endless, and the only limit is your imagination and crochet skills.

Crochet techniques can be used to create a wide variety of projects, including scarves, hats, bags, blankets, and even garments like sweaters or dresses. The deconstructed fabric can be used as the base for these projects, with additional yarn or thread added as needed to complete the design. This combination of upcycled fabric and crochet creates a unique and sustainable piece that is both functional and visually appealing.

One of the benefits of using crochet in the repair and upcycling process is that it allows for flexibility and customization. Crochet stitches can be easily adjusted to accommodate different fabric weights and textures, and the size and shape of the projects can be tailored to fit individual preferences. This means that each upcycled garment or accessory created through this process is truly one-of-a-kind.

In addition to the creative and aesthetic benefits, upcycling garments with crochet also has environmental advantages.

Cleaning and Preparing Clothes for Crochet Work: Cleaning and preparing clothes for crochet work is an essential step in ensuring the quality and longevity of the final product. Whether you are repurposing old garments or starting from scratch with new fabric, taking the time to properly clean and prepare the material will greatly enhance your crochet experience.

Firstly, it is important to assess the condition of the clothes you plan to use. If you are working with second-hand garments, check for any stains, tears, or signs of wear. Stains can be treated with appropriate stain removers or by soaking the garment in a mixture of water and mild detergent. For tears or holes, consider patching them up or cutting around the damaged area to salvage usable fabric.

Once you have addressed any issues with the clothes, it is time to give them a thorough cleaning. This can be done by either hand-washing or machine-washing, depending on the fabric type and your personal preference. Delicate fabrics such as silk or lace should be hand-washed to avoid any damage, while sturdier materials like cotton or denim can withstand machine-washing.

When hand-washing, fill a basin or sink with lukewarm water and add a small amount of gentle detergent. Gently agitate the clothes in the soapy water, paying extra attention to any stained areas. Rinse the garments thoroughly with clean water until all the soap residue is gone. Avoid wringing or twisting the fabric, as this can cause stretching or distortion. Instead, gently squeeze out excess water and lay the clothes flat on a clean towel to dry.

For machine-washing, it is important to select the appropriate cycle and water temperature for the fabric. Use a mild detergent and avoid overloading the machine to ensure proper cleaning. Once the cycle is complete, remove the clothes promptly to prevent wrinkles and hang them up or lay them flat to dry.

After the clothes have been cleaned, it is time to prepare them for crochet work. This involves ironing or steaming the fabric to remove any wrinkles and create a smooth surface for crocheting. Set the iron or steamer to the appropriate temperature for the fabric type and gently press or steam the clothes, being careful not to apply too much heat or pressure. If necessary, use a pressing cloth or towel to protect delicate fabrics from direct contact with the iron.

Once the clothes are clean and prepared, you are ready to start your crochet project.

Celebrating Repairs Clothes: Choosing Colors and Patterns Crochet: When it comes to celebrating repairs clothes, one of the most creative and satisfying ways to do so is by choosing colors and patterns for crochet. Crochet is a versatile and popular craft that allows you to create beautiful and unique designs using yarn and a crochet hook. By incorporating crochet into your clothing repairs, you not only give new life to your garments but also add a personal touch that reflects your style and creativity.

Choosing the right colors for your crochet repairs is essential in achieving a cohesive and visually appealing result. You can opt for colors that match or complement the original garment, or you can go for contrasting colors to create a bold and eye-catching effect. Consider the overall look and feel you want to achieve and select colors accordingly. For example, if you're repairing a summer dress, you might choose bright and vibrant colors to enhance its playful and cheerful vibe. On the other hand, if you're fixing a cozy sweater, you might opt for warm and earthy tones to maintain its cozy and comforting appeal.

Patterns play a crucial role in crochet repairs as they add texture and visual interest to the repaired areas. There are countless crochet stitch patterns to choose from, ranging from simple and basic stitches to intricate and complex designs. The choice of pattern depends on the level of difficulty you're comfortable with and the desired outcome. For a subtle and understated repair, you might opt for a basic stitch pattern such as single crochet or double crochet. These stitches provide a clean and uniform look that seamlessly blends with the original fabric. On the other hand, if you want to make a statement and showcase your crochet skills, you can experiment with more intricate patterns such as cables, lace, or even colorwork.

Incorporating crochet into your clothing repairs not only allows you to fix damaged areas but also gives you the opportunity to add decorative elements and embellishments. You can crochet flowers, appliques, or even intricate motifs to cover up stains, holes, or tears. These embellishments not only serve a functional purpose but also add a touch of uniqueness and creativity to your repaired garment. Additionally, you can use crochet to create edgings or trims to give a finished and polished look to the repaired areas.

The process of celebrating repairs clothes through choosing colors and patterns for crochet is not only a practical solution but also a form of self-expression and creativity. It allows you to transform your damaged garments into one-of-a-kind pieces that reflect your personal style and taste.

Techniques for Intentional Design in Mending of Repair Clothes with Crochet

Mending and repairing clothes is an essential skill that not only helps to extend the lifespan of our garments but also promotes sustainability and reduces waste. One popular technique for mending clothes is using crochet, a versatile and creative craft that allows for intentional design in the repair process.

Crochet is a method of creating fabric by interlocking loops of yarn or thread using a crochet hook. It is a technique that can be easily learned and applied to various types of clothing repairs. When it comes to intentional design in mending clothes with crochet, there are several techniques and approaches that can be employed.

One technique is to use crochet to create decorative patches or appliques to cover up holes or tears in the fabric. This not only serves the purpose of mending the garment but also adds a unique and personalized touch to the design. By choosing different colors, textures, and patterns of yarn, one can create visually appealing patches that enhance the overall aesthetic of the garment.

Another technique is to use crochet to reinforce weak or worn-out areas of the fabric. This can be done by crocheting stitches around the edges of the damaged area, creating a sturdy and durable border that prevents further unraveling or tearing. By using a contrasting color of yarn, this reinforcement can also serve as a decorative element, adding an intentional design element to the repair.

Crochet can also be used to add embellishments or decorative details to clothes that are still in good condition but need a little extra something. This can include crocheting lace trims along the edges of sleeves or hems, adding crochet flowers or motifs to plain garments, or even creating intricate crochet patterns on pockets or collars. These intentional design elements not only enhance the overall look of the garment but also make it unique and personalized.

In addition to the techniques mentioned above, there are countless other ways to incorporate intentional design in mending clothes with crochet. The key is to approach each repair with creativity and an open mind, considering the possibilities that crochet can offer. By experimenting with different stitches, yarns, and techniques, one can create beautiful and functional repairs that transform damaged clothes into unique and stylish pieces.

Overall, using crochet as a technique for intentional design in mending clothes allows for both functionality and creativity. It not only repairs and extends the lifespan of garments but also adds a personal touch and unique design element to each piece.

Incorporating Crochet Patches and Appliqués in Repair Clothes with Crochet: Incorporating crochet patches and appliqués in repairing clothes with crochet is a creative and sustainable way to breathe new life into worn-out garments. Crochet, a versatile and intricate craft, allows for endless possibilities when it comes to mending and embellishing clothing.

Crochet patches are a fantastic solution for covering up holes, tears, or stains on garments. By using a crochet hook and yarn, you can create patches in various shapes and sizes to match the damaged area. Whether it's a small hole on a sweater or a larger tear on a pair of jeans, crochet patches can be customized to seamlessly blend with the fabric, making the repair virtually invisible.

Not only do crochet patches serve a practical purpose, but they also add a unique and personalized touch to the repaired garment. You can experiment with different crochet stitches, patterns, and colors to create eye-catching designs that transform a simple repair into a fashionable statement. For example, you could incorporate a floral motif on a patch to add a touch of femininity to a denim jacket or use geometric patterns to give a modern twist to a plain t-shirt.

In addition to patches, crochet appliqués are another fantastic way to repair and enhance clothing. Appliqués are small crochet motifs that can be sewn or attached to garments to cover up imperfections or add decorative elements. They can be made in various shapes, such as flowers, animals, or abstract designs, and can be easily customized to suit your personal style.

Crochet appliqués offer endless possibilities for creativity and self-expression. You can mix and match different motifs to create unique combinations or use them to tell a story or convey a message through your clothing. For example, you could create a patchwork of crochet appliqués representing different travel destinations on a backpack, showcasing your love for adventure and exploration.

One of the great advantages of incorporating crochet patches and appliqués in repairing clothes is the sustainability aspect. Instead of discarding damaged garments and contributing to the fast fashion cycle, crochet repairs allow you to extend the lifespan of your clothing and reduce waste. By embracing this craft, you can actively participate in the slow fashion movement and promote a more sustainable and conscious approach to fashion.

Furthermore, crochet repairs offer a sense of empowerment and self-sufficiency. Learning how to mend and embellish your clothes with crochet not only saves you money but also gives you the ability to take control of your wardrobe.

HACKING:
A WAY OF LIFE

This book is not just a collection of crochet patterns or a selection of makes and hacks to keep you looking 'de rigeur'. Oh no! This book is actually a toolkit of hints, tips and instructions to help you rethink the clothes that are already around you, from your own wardrobe to second-hand stores and thrifted finds. This book is a way of life.

NEW JEANS
60 WATTS ENERGY
2180 LTR WATER
CO2 OF 5KM CAR JOURNEY

2ND HAND JEANS
82% LESS IMPACT

There are already enough clothes in the world. Fact. Every year 80 billion new garments are sold; that is a HUGE amount. When you get to thinking about how many plants have to be grown, watered, sprayed with pesticides, processed into fabric, cut, sewn, pressed, and then shipped around the world to get to a high street shop near you, it's mind boggling.

Add that to the fact that most people throw away half a kilo of clothes a year. Each. Even if you donate yours to charity, only 10% are actually bought and rehoused and the rest can still end up in landfill giving off methane and could take 200 years to break down, or get sent overseas for someone else to deal with. This, my friends, is a big part of the climate crisis and to make a difference we need to either keep the clothes we have or buy second-hand clothes.

But this is not a book to make you feel guilty about that. In fact, this book is the opposite. This is for people that **love** clothes. Keeping them for longer definitely helps; a garment kept for over three years will reduce its global impact by 20–30%. But buying something second-hand instead of new will reduce the carbon footprint by a whopping 82%. So, I'm not talking about mending stuff to make sure it lives longer, I'm talking about **remaking** stuff. Seeing the potential in second-hand and remodelling, remaking and changing it to make it something you truly love.

NEW V SECOND HAND

This book is for people that want to rehabilitate ill-fitting t-shirts and make them functioning members of society again. It's for people that want to fall back in love with jackets and jumpers that have been lying at the bottom of drawers and hanging in the back of cupboards. Using a bit of crochet, scissors and some simple stitches this book of crochet hacking will show you how to completely rethink your relationship to clothes, inspire you to say yes to preloved, save things from landfill and make real change in the world.

CROCHET
HACKING
STARTER KIT

There are only a few things you'll need to get crochet hacking and the first is probably the most important.

CONFIDENCE

More than anything, don't be afraid of cutting into your clothes. It can be terrifying at first, we're not used to interacting with our wardrobes like this, but people used to do this **all** the time. Almost any mis-cut can be fixed with a bit of wool and some lateral thinking, and at the very worst you'll have learned how *not* to do something. You **can** do this!

FABRIC SCISSORS

For almost everything in this book I would say 'use it as a guide, not a rule'. Except for this one. Cutting up fabric with a little pair of scissors that you find in the kitchen drawer will never be ok. Go on, try it, right now. Found some? Ok, grab any old thing and try and make a nice cut. Doesn't work, does it? It will be really hard work and the end result will be raggedy. Proper fabric scissors will cut like a dream, leave a lovely smooth finish and leave your hacks looking as professional as possible.

EMBROIDERY NEEDLE

I will happily use any needle I have to hand. A yarn needle is a great size but can make it hard work when sewing into fabric. A large eye embroidery needle will take most yarns and make hand sewing a bit easier.

CROCHET HOOKS

This is a given, but you will notice that I sometimes recommend using a smaller hook than is usual for the yarn weight. This is because it makes a slightly denser crochet fabric, and when you're working into jersey or wool you want to try to keep the crochet elements from stretching out too much. I often use a mix of yarn weights too, so I find working with a hook that fits the lighter weight yarn tends to be my preferred approach, but experiment and see what works for you.

BODKIN

This is also called a bradawl and is just a long pointy tool used in leather work. They are really inexpensive and having tried a number of things to make holes in fabric this is definitely the best. That said, I often use a large sewing needle and then widen the hole with a knitting needle.

LEATHER PUNCH

I have also used a leather punch to make holes in fabric that my husband bought years ago when he was going through a leather working phase (he's an engineer with a tool obsession, I assume they all go through a similar phase at some point) and it's ideal for using on denim.

WASHABLE PEN
Used to mark where holes are needed on your fabric.

YARN
STASH

Usually when you go through a process of creating patterns for people, you'll choose a brand of yarn that you know is available to buy, buy it in the colours you want to recommend, make the pattern and share the instructions. But this isn't just a book of crochet patterns, this is a hacking, remaking toolkit and we need to think about the role yarn has to play in it.

Most commercial yarn is now made with acrylic. Acrylic has lots of great features; it is durable, flexible, washable, soft and cheap; it is hypoallergenic, reusable and versatile. It is also made of plastic which means it doesn't rot down like wool or cotton but stays around for hundreds of years. I also have heaps of it. I mean **heaps**.

In an ideal world all of these hacks would use sustainably sourced yarns, from ethically farmed wool to organic cottons, and if you have the opportunity to work with these materials then so much the better. But rather than encouraging you to go out and buy yet more yarn I suggest you take this opportunity to use up any yarns that you have already. Mixing DK (Light Worsted) and Aran (Worsted) or Chunky (Bulky) and Aran (Worsted) is going to make very little difference to the overall finish and fit of things. All of the makes in this book have been created with leftovers from my yarn stash and I happily mix cottons with acrylic or wool with bamboo. In crochet hacking anything goes as long as the colours make you happy and they fit on the same hook.

For each of the patterns in this book I have shared the weight of the wool and the hook size I've used, but these are just suggestions. I have also mixed up brands, materials, colours and weights so will often not specify who made it or where it came from. The only real guideline which is helpful to remember is that a Chunky (Bulky) or Aran (Worsted) weight yarn is good for use on a heavy weight fabric, like a sweater or wool garment, and a DK (Light Worsted) or lightweight yarn is good for use on a lighter weight fabric like a t-shirt. That's it!

DENIM

DENIM IS THE ROCK LEGEND OF CLOTHING, IT JUST KEEPS COMING BACK WITH HIT AFTER HIT.

Denim made its debut as workwear in the 1870s and over time has been transformed from it's origins as simple, labourers' overalls to serious, high-end couture. Most of us will have at least one denim item in our wardrobe, and many of us will wear something made from denim every day. In fact, every year 450 million pairs of jeans are sold in the US alone, and a study in 2015 found that the average woman owns seven pairs of jeans but actually only wears four of them.

BUT WHY THE LOVE AFFAIR? AND WHAT HAPPENS WHEN WE'VE HAD ENOUGH OF ALL THOSE JEANS?

Denim is made from cotton, traditionally woven with one thread dyed with indigo and the other left white and compared to other fabrics, cotton is pretty cheap to make. What makes denim jeans different from a cotton shirt is that the material is often woven from a much thicker spun yarn and will be held together with rivets. This makes denim an incredibly durable fabric and is one of the reasons we love it so much.

You'd think that being a natural material is a **good** thing, and it is, but the flip side is that cotton uses a huge amount of resources when grown, and unless it's organically farmed and grown it's really not that great. If it's been mixed with any other material like the lycra in your skinny jeans it'll take a long time to decompose and all of the textiles that end up in landfill create huge amounts of methane that are contributing to global warming. So what does any **Rock Legend** worth her salt do? She reinvents herself.

Denim is a brilliant fabric to crochet with because it's so tough. You can cut it into any shape you like and by using a leather punch or just a good sharp knitting needle, you can make holes around the edges to work into. This gives you the versatility to make patches, change edges and alter shapes. This collection of denim crochet hacks is here to inspire you; as with all of the projects in this book they are suggestions and ideas, and as denim is so durable you can keep reshaping and remaking it as long as you like.

HOW TO WORK CROCHET INTO DENIM

To crochet hack denim, all you have to do is make holes in it and crochet directly into the material. First you need to decide if you have thick or thin denim. If you think your material is tough enough to work into without fraying, then it's thick. If it feels a bit on the floppy side or is well worn and prone to fraying then it's thin. If it's thin and you are sewing it you would hem the edge of your fabric to stop it from fraying, but this is crochet hacking and we like to keep things simple so all you need is an iron and some hemming tape, and then you can work into it just as you would with thick denim.

TOOLS

To make the holes you need either a bradawl or a sharp knitting needle or even a big embroidery needle can work well. You can also use a leather punch, which works just like a hole punch and makes working through waistbands and very thick material super easy.

TECHNIQUES

WORKING CROCHET INTO DENIM

The spacing of the holes will be dependent on the thickness of the yarn you want to use and the size of the hook, so it's always a good idea to whip up a little sample and use it as a template. Here's how to do it.

STEP 1
Ch12.
Row 1: tr into 3rd ch from hook, tr into each ch to the end.

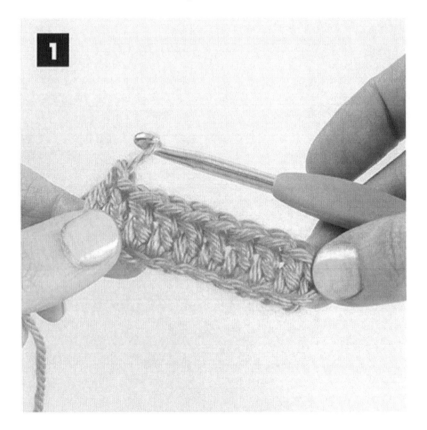

STEP 2
Using a washable pen, make a mark on your material every 2 stitches using the crochet sample as a template.

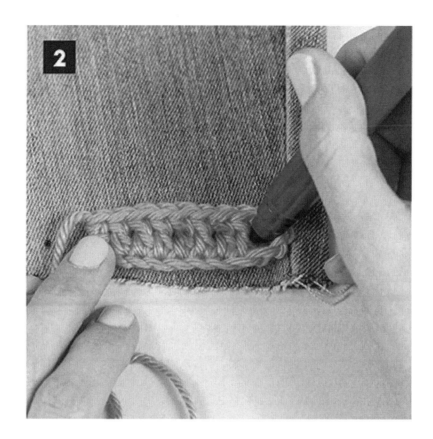

STEP 3
Make holes in the fabric using whatever tool you have to hand. I really recommend investing in a leather punch; mine has come in so handy.

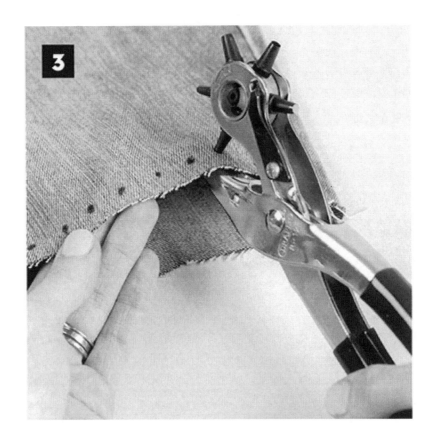

STEP 4
You can use a knitting needle or a bradawl to make the holes bigger if required.

STEP 5
Insert your crochet hook into the first hole, draw up a loop and work 2 chain stitches (these are not counted as a st).

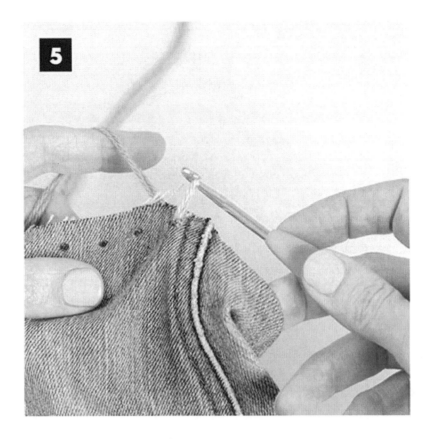

STEP 6

Work 2dc in each hole. Continue to crochet, using the holes as your stitches. This illustration shows working 2dc in each hole, as the distance taken from the template was 2 stitches apart.

If you wanted to do this with thin denim, first fold over the cut edge, hem with tape by following the instructions on the tape you have and then follow the above technique.

You can take a much more cavalier approach, by making some holes and seeing how many stitches fit nicely between each hole. This usually takes a bit longer and can involve ripping back an hour's worth of crochet but we have all the time in the world, so who cares?

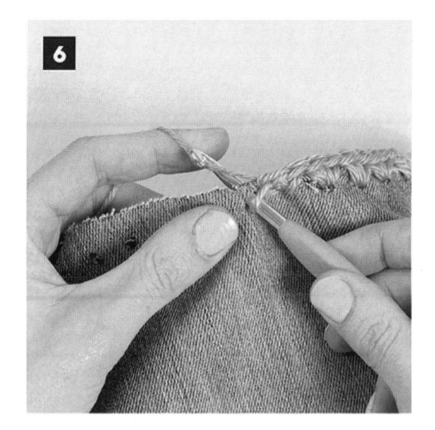

Did you know: It takes the same amount of energy to make a new pair of jeans as it would to have the TV on for nearly 2 solid weeks. Reusing old ones is so much better!

SPRING STAYCATION JACKET

This year my little sister got married on the very beautiful island of Kos. Not being one that travels much or one that even ventures out when it gets 'slightly warm' my wardrobe was not prepared for this. Rather than buying a whole bunch of new clothes to take with me, I decided to see if I could remake what I needed with things I already had at home and from my local second-hand stores. As soon as I found this extra-large man's denim shirt I knew I'd be able to do something with it, and the transformation has become a permanent member of my spring wardrobe.

MATERIALS

- Large denim shirt
- 8mm crochet hook
- Sharp scissors

- Hole making tool
- Yarn needle
- Scrap material for pocket lining
- Washable pen or tailors chalk
- Sewing pins
- Chunky (Bulky) weight yarn in the colour of your choice

If you want to use a different weight yarn, just make sure you have a hook size to match. I used Paintbox Wool Mix Chunky in Primrose.

STITCHES

CROCHET
dc – UK double (US single) crochet
tr – UK treble (US double) crochet
ch – chain
ss – slip stitch
st(s) – stitch(es)

SEWING
Back stitch
Machine straight stitch

HOW TO

STEP 1
Cut off the cuffs and the collar of the shirt. Use the seam lines as a guide.

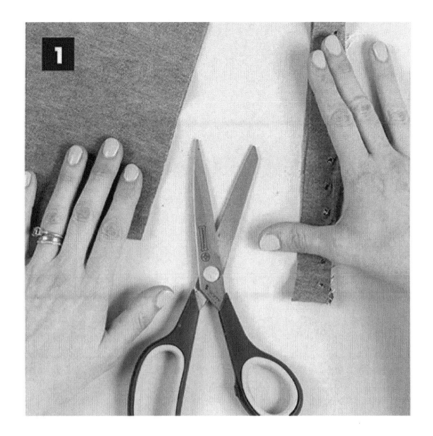

STEP 2
Make a crochet sample in your yarn to create a template, mark and make holes 2 sts apart around the cuff, collar and bottom edges.

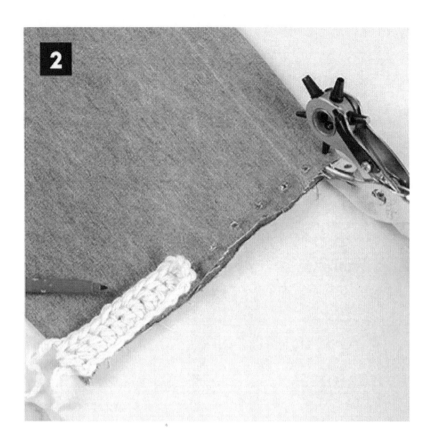

STEP 3

To make the cuffs join in your yarn with 2ch and work 2dc in each hole, ss in first dc to join.

Rounds 1–4: ch2 (does not count as st), tr in each st to the end, ss in first tr.

Repeat for the collar and bottom edge, but working in rows and turning.

STEP 4
You can leave things there if you like, or if you want to add pockets, pop the shirt on and make a mark using a washable pen where you want the pockets to sit. Making sure they are symmetrically placed, make a straight cut about the same width as your hand. Use the width of your cut as the measurement for the width of your pocket lining. To make the pocket lining cut 2 rectangles for each pocket, trim one end to create a curve and sew together around sides and curve, leaving the straight top edge open. You can do this by hand with back stitch or with a sewing machine.

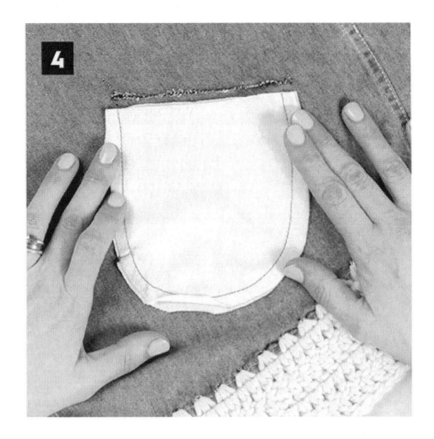

STEP 5

On the inside of the shirt, tack the pocket in place with pins and sew one open edge to the top of the straight cut and the other to the bottom. This can be a bit fiddly, but once you have crocheted a new edge no one will see a thing!

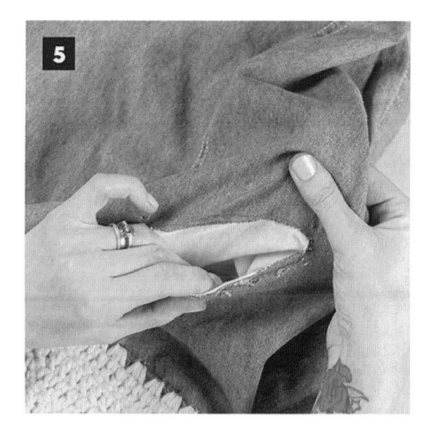

STEP 6
Using your crochet template, mark and make holes 2 sts apart along the bottom pocket edge. Join yarn with 2ch and crochet 2dc in each st. Finish the edge with a row of tr and fasten off.

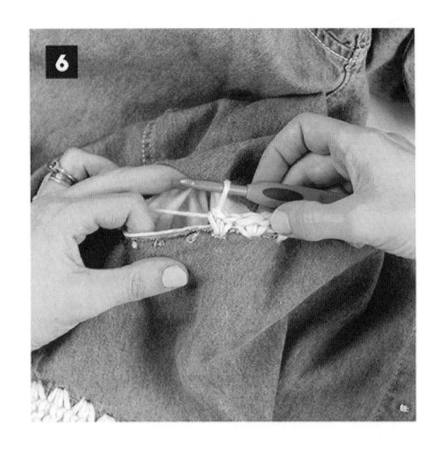

NOT YOUR GRANNY'S BOMBER

This badass beauty takes the classic granny square and turns it into a modern masterpiece. It started life as a man's denim shirt and some granny squares that had been languishing in my WIP pile, waiting to be turned into a blanket. With a bit of rejigging and thinking about them in a different way, this jacket/jumper/shirt now has a new life and pride of place in my wardrobe. This bit of hacking works best with a sewing machine to make the new waistband, but feel free to experiment with a different style waistband that suits your skills and comfort level.

MATERIALS

- Denim shirt
- 5mm crochet hook
- Sharp scissors

- Sewing machine
- Measuring tape
- 2.5m by 1cm (2.8yds x $^1/_2$in) wide elastic
- Safety pin
- Aran (Worsted) weight yarn in colours of your choice

If you want to use a different weight yarn, just make sure you have a hook size to match. You might find that you need an extra row in your granny square if you go for a lighter weight yarn. I used a mix of Cascade Pacific and Caron Simply Soft.

STITCHES

CROCHET
dc – UK double (US single) crochet
tr – UK treble (US double) crochet
ch – chain
ch sp – chain space
ss – slip stitch
st(s) – stitch(es)

SEWING
Back stitch
Whip stitch
Machine straight stitch

HOW TO

STEP 1
Turn the shirt inside out and fold up the waist until it sits at the height that you want it. From the fold, measure and mark out lines 2cm ($^3/_4$in) apart to make 3 channels. These channels will hold the elastic. Use a sewing machine to sew along the lines.

STEP 2

Cut the elastic into 3 lengths. Use your waist as a guide to make them a length that sits comfortably. I have a size UK 8 to 10 (US 6 to 8) waist and my elastic lengths were 75cm (29^1/$_2$in) each. Pop the safety pin on one end of a piece of elastic and feed it through one of the channels. Secure at either end with a little bit of stitching and repeat for the other channels.

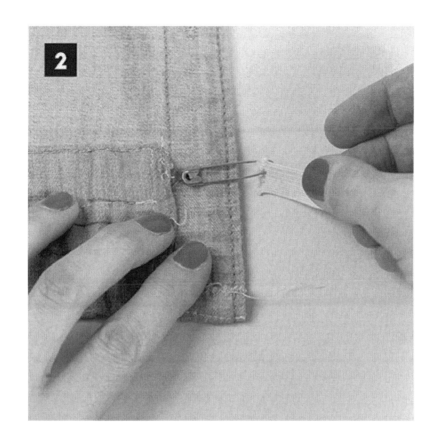

STEP 3
Cut off the collar and sleeves and remove the cuffs from the ends.
You'll need these later on.

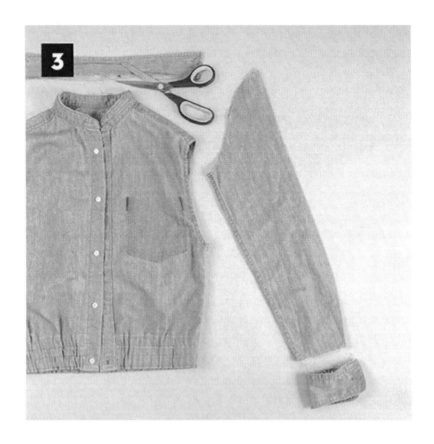

STEP 4

Make 14 granny squares in one colour, and 8 in multiple colours –
changing colour on each round. Make 4 half granny squares in
multiple colours.

GRANNY

The pattern shows where to use the different colours for the multiple
colour granny squares. When working the single colour squares just
continue with the same colour throughout.
Using yarn A, ch4, ss in first ch to make a loop.
Round 1: working into the loop using yarn A, ch3 (counts as tr), 2tr,
ch2, (3tr, ch2) 3 times, ss to top of ch3, fasten off.
Round 2: using yarn B, work [ch3, tr] in first ch sp, work tr in each st
around edge and [2tr, ch2, 2tr] in each corner ch-sp to first ch sp,
[2tr, ch2, ss to top of ch3] in first ch sp to finish, fasten off.
Rounds 3–4: work as for round 2 using yarns C, then D.
Round 5: using yarn E, work ch2 in first ch sp (counts as first dc),
work dc in each st around edge and [dc, ch2, dc] in each corner ch sp
to first ch sp, [dc, ch2, ss to top of ch2] in first ch sp to finish, fasten
off.
Weave in all ends.

HALF GRANNY

Using yarn A, ch4, ss in first ch to make a loop.
Row 1: working into the loop using yarn A, ch3 (counts as tr), 2tr, ch2, 3tr, turn, fasten off.
Row 2: using yarn B, work [ch3, tr] in same st, tr in each st to ch sp, [2tr, 2ch, 2tr] in ch sp, tr in each st to last st, 2tr in last st, turn, fasten off.
Rows 3–4: work as for row 2 using yarns C, then D.
Row 5: using yarn E, ch2 (counts as first dc), dc in each st to ch sp, [dc, ch2, dc] in ch sp, dc in each st to end, ch2, dc evenly along bottom edge of triangle by working around the posts of the sts, ch2, ss to top of ch2 to finish, fasten off.
Weave in all ends.

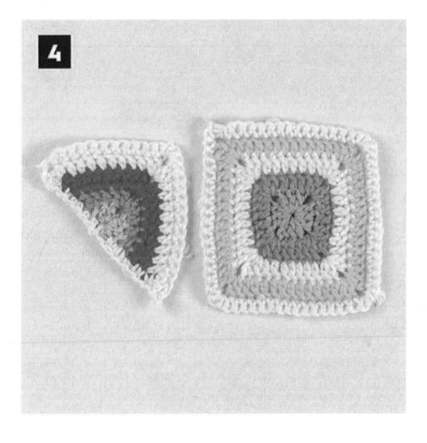

STEP 5
Lay out the finished squares as illustrated and sew together using whip stitch.

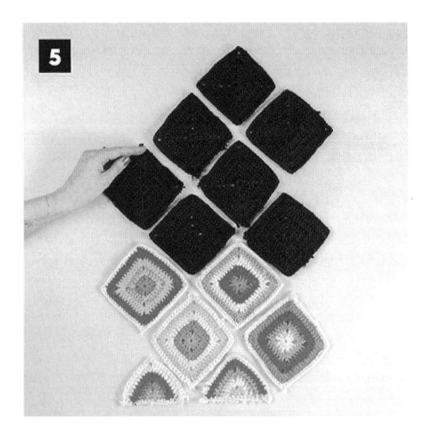

STEP 6

Sew all edges together to make a tube. Join yarn E at the edge of the cuff and work 3 rounds of dc. Join the yarn used for the single colour grannies to the top of the sleeve and work 3 rounds of dc.

STEP 7

Use a back stitch to attach the sleeve to the body of the shirt.

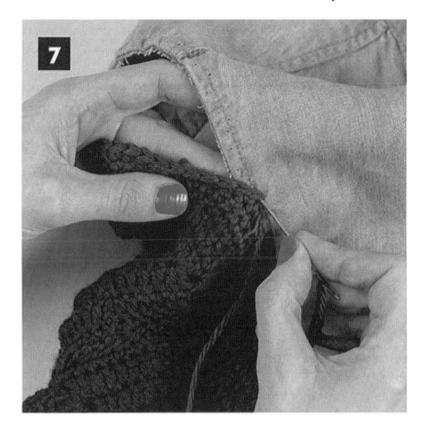

STEP 8
Use a back stitch to reattach the cuffs to the end of the sleeves. This can be a little fiddly but is worth persevering as it's a nice finishing touch.

SASHIKO STITCHED DUNGAREES

This make is inspired by a pair of jeans that I can't let go of and the Japanese art of Sashiko stitching. Sashiko is a style of practical, reinforcement stitching used in mending, and every time my jeans get a hole they get another patch or spot of sashiko. After using a pocket from a worn out (too short!) mini skirt as a patch, I was left with a pile of denim elements that were perfect for transforming into dungarees. These instructions will vary depending on the sizes of the pockets you have to work around, the style and shape of your jeans, the width of your waistband, all sorts of things! You may want less rows around the bib and more for the straps, just keep experimenting until you find something that works for you.

MATERIALS

- An old denim mini skirt, or anything with pockets and a waist band
- 3.5mm crochet hook
- Sharp scissors

- Hole making tool
- Yarn needle
- Needle and thread
- Small buttons
- DK (Light Worsted) weight yarn in colours of your choice

I used Scheepjes Soft Fun DK Yarn and a 3.5mm hook as I wanted quite a dense fabric to match the weight of the denim.

STITCHES

CROCHET
dc – UK double (US single) crochet
tr – UK treble (US double) crochet
tr2tog – work 2 UK trebles (US doubles) together to make one stitch
ch – chain
ch sp – chain space
ss – slip stitch
st(s) – stitch(es)

SEWING
Back stitch
Whip stitch

HOW TO

MAKE THE BIB

STEP 1
Cut the back pocket out of the mini skirt (use the other to patch your jeans!) leaving approx 1.5cm ($^1/_2$in) width around the outside. Make a sample of crochet to use as a template and mark out holes for every third stitch. Work all around the edge of the pocket making the same number of holes on the top, bottom and side edges – this will ensure that your crochet is symmetrical.

STEP 2

Join yarn in one corner hole. Change colours after a complete round whenever you want to.

Round 1: [ch3 (counts as tr), ch2, 3tr] in same hole, (3tr in each hole to the corner hole, [3tr, ch2, 3tr] in the corner hole) 3 times, 3tr in each hole to the corner hole, 2tr in the corner hole, ss to top of ch3 to join, ss into ch sp.

Round 2: repeat round 1, working in the gaps between 3tr groups and in the corner ch sps.

Rounds 3–5: working in side edges and bottom edge only, [ch3, tr] in same ch sp, (3tr in each gap between 3tr groups to corner ch sp, [3tr, ch2, 3tr] in corner ch sp) twice, 3tr in each gap between 3tr groups to corner ch sp, 2tr in corner ch sp, turn.

Round 6: working in side edges and bottom edge only, ch3 (counts as tr), tr in each st along side, [2tr, ch2, 2tr] in corner ch sp, 3tr in each gap between 3tr groups along bottom edge, [2tr, ch2, 2tr] in corner ch sp, tr in each st along side. Fasten off yarn.

Rounds 7–9: working in bottom edge only, rejoin yarn, [ch3, tr] in first st, 3tr in each gap between 3tr groups, 2tr in last st, turn.

Round 10: ch1 (does not count as st), dc in each st around the whole of the square, with [2dc, ch2, 2dc] in each corner ch sp.

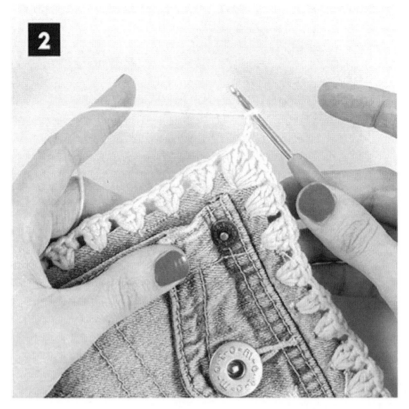

MAKE THE TOP EDGE

STEP 3

Making sure that you include the buttonhole, cut a strip of the waist band from the mini skirt to the same width as the top of the crochet bib. Line up against the crochet square, mark and make holes every third stitch.

Join yarn in the first hole [ch3, 2tr] in first hole then work 3tr in each hole, fasten off.

Whip stitch to the top of the square.

Making sure you include the button this time, cut another length of old waistband so that it fits from one side of the bib, around your neck and buttons up comfortably in the buttonhole. Hand stitch the ends together to secure the strap – you will now be able to use the button to take your dungarees on and off.

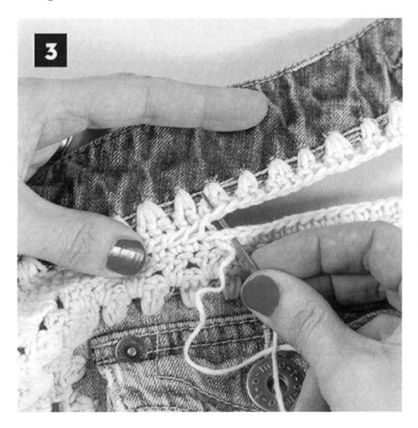

STEP 4

Back stitch edge of bib to the top of the jeans, covering up the button of the existing fly.

MAKE THE BACK STRAPS

STEP 5

The neck strap you just made? You can either leave this as the finished strap or you can make a more traditional back strap. Cut a length of denim that is the same width as the neck strap and sits from the top of the jeans to just below your shoulder blades. Make holes all the way around each edge and work [ch3, 2tr] in first hole and 3tr in each remaining hole. Work a second row of tr in each st.

STEP 6

Now cut the neck strap in half, right down the middle and make 3 holes along the short edge of each half.

On each edge:

Row 1: ch3 (counts as tr) 2tr in same hole, 3tr in next 2 holes, turn. (9 tr)

Rows 2–5: ch2 (does not count as st), tr in each st, turn.

Rows 6–8: ch2 (does not count as st), tr2tog, tr in each st, turn. (6 tr)

In the centre middle of the back of the jeans make 3 holes and repeat row 1 above. Fasten off and whip stitch the long piece of crocheted denim to these stitches. Then whip stitch the top to the crochet you added to the neck strap.

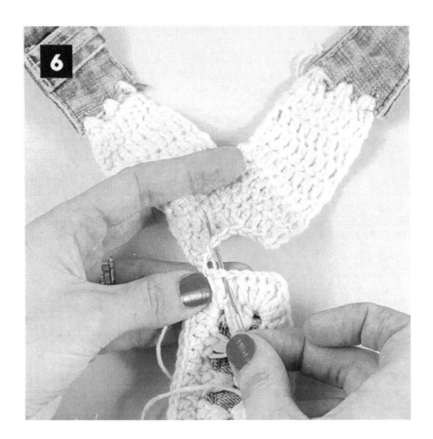

TO MAKE THE BUTTON FLY

STEP 7

Make a cut approximately 10cm (4in) long down the side seam of the jeans. Make holes along each edge, join yarn with 2ch and work 3dc into each hole.

On one edge only, work one row of tr in each st, then one row of dc in each st.

The tr row will become the new buttonholes.

STEP 8

On the other edge sew on small buttons and fasten through the buttonholes. That's it!

PURDY NIFTY LITTLE PURSE

This nifty little purse was made for two reasons. Firstly, because I lost my wallet and figured that it would be quicker, cheaper and a better way of getting a new one to make it myself rather than buying one. Secondly because my eldest son insists on hunting down jeans which are too small for him and wearing them as ankle swingers – he prefers them this way. Cutting up his old, no longer used, holey jeans has killed two birds with one stone.

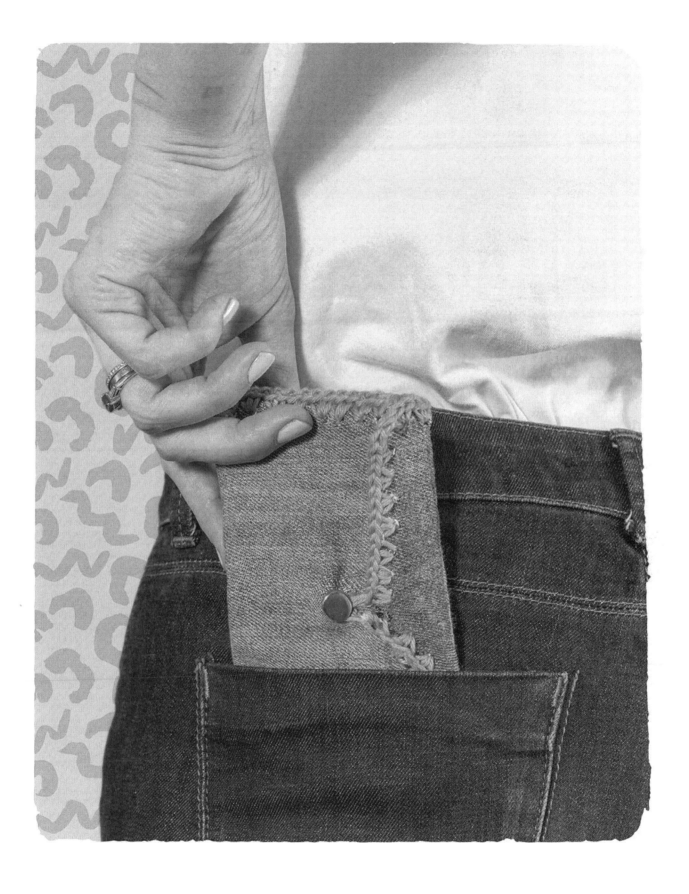

MATERIALS

- Old denim, the back leg of a pair of jeans is ideal
- 4mm crochet hook
- Sharp scissors
- Hole making tool
- Yarn needle
- Button
- Needle and thread
- DK (Light Worsted) cotton yarn in the colour of your choice

If you want to use a different weight yarn, just make sure you have a hook size to match.

STITCHES

CROCHET
dc - UK double (US single) crochet
tr – UK treble (US double) crochet
ch - chain
ss – slip stitch
st(s) – stitch(es)

SEWING
Whip stitch

HOW TO

STEP 1
You can make your purse any shape you like, a simple rectangle is ideal for a beginner or you can get a bit fancy and cut a scalloped edge and add a couple of cut outs at the bottom as I've done here. Make it with a bit of paper first to see how you like it and then use the paper as a template.

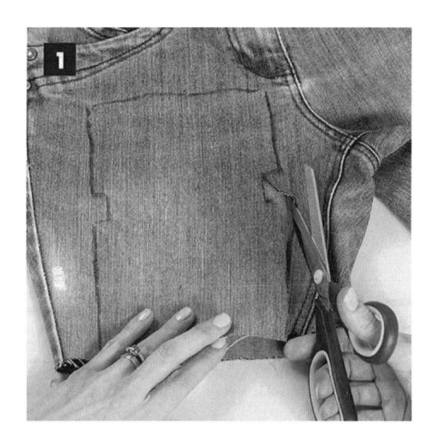

STEP 2
Cut out your denim to make the base for the purse.

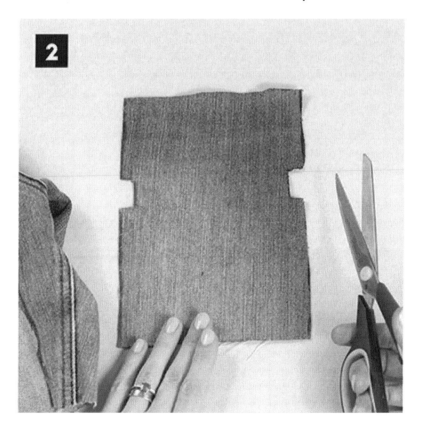

STEP 3

Work a little crochet sample using your yarn of choice and use this as a template to mark out your holes. For this pattern, make a mark every second stitch all around the fabric and then use whatever sharp tool you prefer to make the holes. Join in your yarn with 2ch and work 2dc in each hole, ss in first dc and fasten off to finish.

STEP 4

Fold the fabric so that the cut out sections become the bottom of the wallet and whip stitch the sides together.

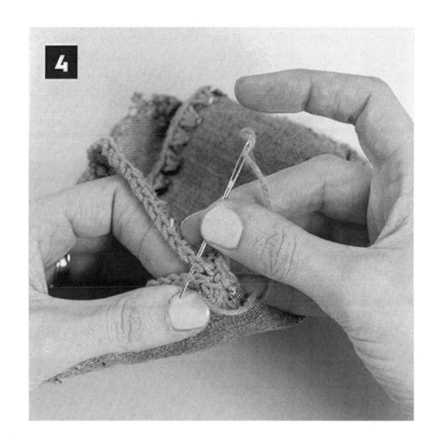

STEP 5
Using a crochet stitch as the buttonhole, mark the position of the button.

STEP 6

Sew on a button to secure your purse when it's closed.

JERSEY

Most high street t-shirts and sweatshirts are made of it. Our bedding, joggers and pyjamas are often made of it. But what exactly is it? Unlike denim, which is woven cotton, jersey is knitted cotton. This can be easier to produce as it just uses one continuous thread and it can give a nice, flexible, stretchy finish; great for if you're looking to mass produce a 'one size fits all' garment. When my Nan was growing up jersey would have been made from wool, but it's now mostly made from a mix of polyester and cotton. Cotton, as we know, is made from plant fibres and is breathable, soft and hypoallergenic, but what is polyester?

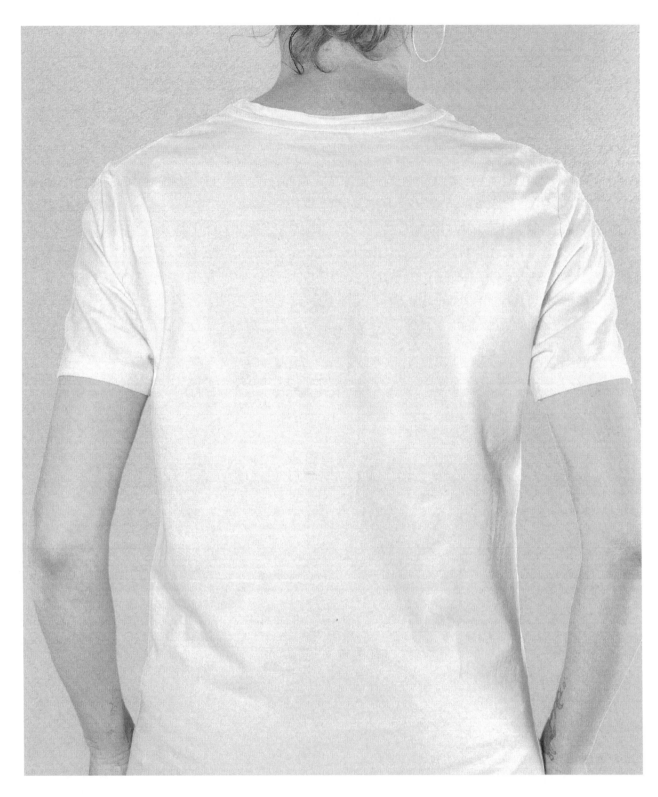

Polyester is made from a chemical reaction involving air, water and petroleum. Yep, the very same petroleum that is processed from crude oil, drilled out of the ground and carted about in massive tankers. It is then processed and turned into a form of plastic. Now plastic can be amazing: it is strong, lasts forever, is flexible, versatile, waterproof and easy to clean. Paired with cotton it can make a t-shirt that is breathable, soft, easy to clean, durable, and cheap to produce. But as part of a fast fashion, high turnover, short term bit of clothing it is a massive problem.

EVERY YEAR 2 BILLION T-SHIRTS ARE SOLD, BUT EVERY YEAR THE AVERAGE PERSON THROWS AWAY 31KG OF CLOTHES, THAT'S THE EQUIVALENT OF 22 T-SHIRTS. AND NOT THROWN AWAY AS IN DONATED TO CHARITY OR GIVEN TO A FRIEND BUT THROWN AWAY AS IN CHUCKED IN THE BIN AND DUMPED IN A LANDFILL. WITH THEIR AMAZING DURABLE QUALITIES THEY STAY THERE, SLOWLY RELEASING METHANE FOR AN EXTREMELY LONG TIME...

However, there is good news: jersey garments are fantastic for remaking. They don't fray when you cut them, they will happily hold new stitches and embellishments without any problems. They can be reshaped, revamped and rehabilitated back into functioning members of society incredibly easily. This chapter will give you a whole heap of ideas that will have you reimagining too tight tees and preloved tops and will show you different techniques to use crochet to transform something old into something new.

HOW TO WORK CROCHET INTO JERSEY

Crocheting into jersey all comes down to hand sewing. You don't need to be an embroidery pro or an Elizabethan seamstress, you just need to get to grips with a simple running stitch or a bit of back stitch. Because jersey doesn't fray, you can usually just cut and stitch without the need for hemming or binding. That said, it always pays to make a little test cut in a hem somewhere to see how the fabric behaves. If it looks like it'll hold then it probably will. The only thing you do need to be aware of is stretching it out of shape or pulling your stitches too tight, but this improves with practise, and if it's a t-shirt that was headed for landfill then using it for a bit of practise isn't going to hurt and you can always add it to your fabric stash and find a way to reuse it later.

TOOLS

A good, sharp embroidery needle is all you need. You ideally want to work your stitches in the same yarn that you intend to use for the first row of crochet, so you need a needle that will have a big enough eye to take the yarn, but a pointy enough end to make sewing easy.

When attaching a finished piece of crochet onto a piece of clothing you may also want to invest in some yarn pins. They have a larger head than regular fabric pins and will allow you to line things up just right before you get sewing.

TECHNIQUES

WORKING CROCHET INTO RUNNING STITCH

STEP 1

Thread the needle, tie a knot in the end and insert the needle in the back of the fabric around 1cm (1/2in) from the cut edge. Work a few running stitches.

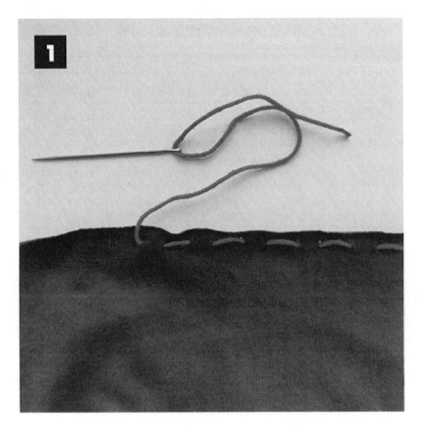

STEP 2

Insert the crochet hook under the first stitch, draw up a loop of yarn and ch1 (this does not count as a st), dc in the same stitch, dc in the next stitch. Depending on the thickness of the yarn and size of the running stitch, you may need to work 1, 2 or 3 dc stitches in each running stitch to create a crochet edge that lays flat and does not stretch or pucker.

Repeat the above steps, working a few running stitches followed by a few crochet stitches. Working in this way allows you to keep the right tension on the jersey. Keep going until you reach the end and fasten off the yarn.

Working into back stitch is just the same process: work a few back stitches, crochet around them and make sure that the tension isn't too tight or too loose. Each pattern will indicate whether you use a dc or a tr as the crochet stitch, and that's it!

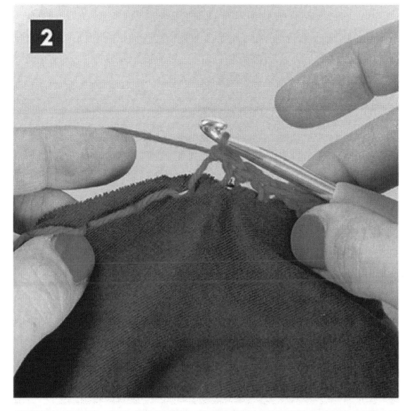

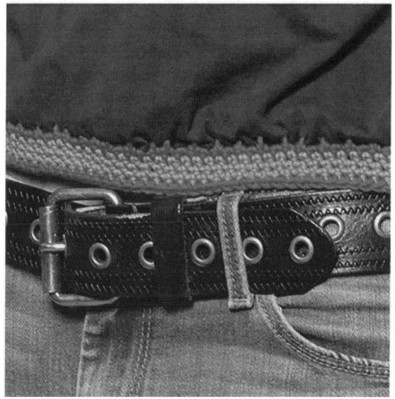

HAND SEWING CROCHET ONTO A GARMENT

STEP 1

Pin the crochet in place on the garment.Use the same colour yarn as the crochet and secure in place with a back stitch worked between each crochet stitch. If you're more comfortable using a running stitch that's fine, but the finish won't be quite as smooth. Make sure you don't pull the stitches too tight.

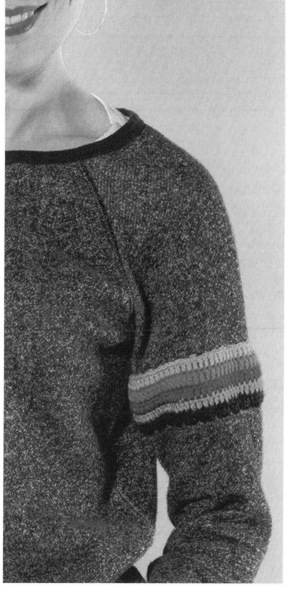

Did you know: The Fashion and Textile industry is the 2nd biggest polluter on the planet, and collectively we consume 400% more clothes than we did in the year 2000.

HOT SAUCE
T-SHIRT
DRESS

This is a really simple transformation to turn a large t-shirt into a summer dress. I like a low neckline, but you can leave yours as it is or go all out and make it off the shoulder, whatever works for you.

MATERIALS

- Large T-shirt
- 4.5mm crochet hook
- Large eye embroidery needle
- Sharp scissors
- Yarn needle
- Aran (Worsted) weight cotton

STITCHES

CROCHET
dc – UK double (US single) crochet
tr – UK treble (US double) crochet
ch – chain
ss – slip stitch
st(s) – stitch(es)

SEWING
Back stitch

HOW TO

STEP 1
The best way to keep your cutting neat and symmetrical is to fold the t-shirt in half lengthways before cutting. Cut the neckline to the desired shape using the existing neckline as a guide. Cut approximately 25cm (10in) from the bottom and put the bottom section to one side.

STEP 2

Using the cotton and the embroidery needle work a row of running stitches along the edge of the neck. To keep the tee from puckering up, sew a few stitches but don't fasten off the yarn. Join in same colour yarn with 1ch and work 1 to 2dc in each st, continue like this to the end, ss in first dc to finish. You'll need to experiment to get the tension right.

Next round: ch1 (does not count as st), 1dc in each st, ss in first dc to join and fasten off.

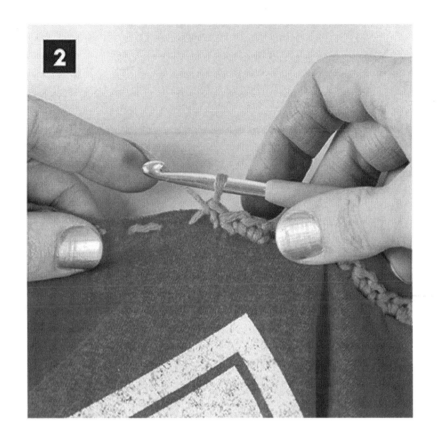

STEP 3
Repeat step 2 along the cut edge of the tee.
Next round: ch2 (does not count as st), tr in each st, ss in first tr to join.
Repeat the last round until you have the desired length; I worked 7 rounds.
Final round: ch1, dc in each st, ss in first dc to join and fasten off.

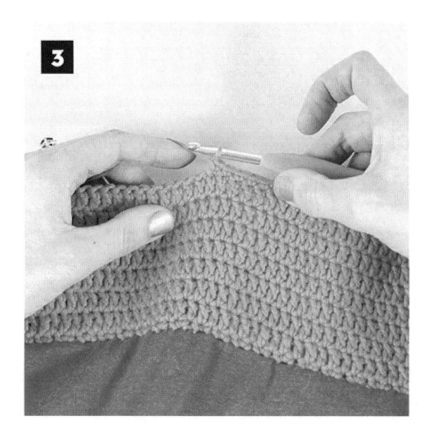

STEP 4
Using yarn needle and thread reattach the bottom part of the tee.

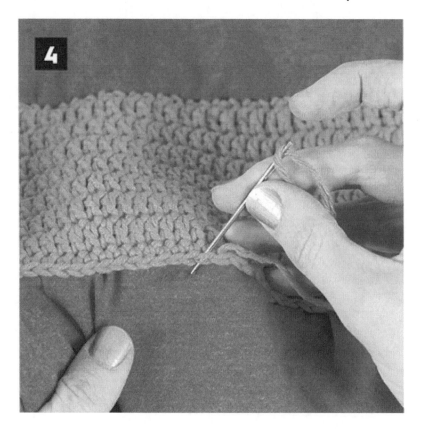

STEP 5
Cut 1m (1.1yds) length of yarn and weave through the top row of tr to use as a drawstring.

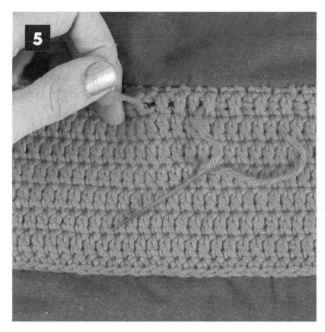

ROCK 'N' ROSES CROP TOP

While crochet hacking is about thinking of new ways to remake existing clothes, it's also about mending. This tee had a hair dye incident and got a big bleached patch on the bottom at the back. Having had it for a long time I was loathe to get rid of it so I chopped off the bleached bit and revamped the neckline so that it can have a whole new life.

MATERIALS

- T-shirt
- 4mm crochet hook
- Large eye embroidery needle

- Sharp scissors
- Washable pen or tailors chalk
- DK (Light Worsted) weight yarn in two colours

I used a DK cotton but you can use any yarn you like. A DK weight is better for this kind of transformation as it isn't too bulky.

STITCHES

CROCHET
dc – UK double (US single) crochet
tr – UK treble (US double) crochet
ch – chain
ss – slip stitch
st(s) – stitch(es)

SEWING
Back stitch

HOW TO

STEP 1
To cut the bottom, fold the t-shirt in half lengthways and cut at the desired height. It's worth trying it on first and making a mark with a washable pen or tailors chalk so that you don't make it too short. To cut the neck, make a snip through and cut around following the ribbed jersey of the neckline.

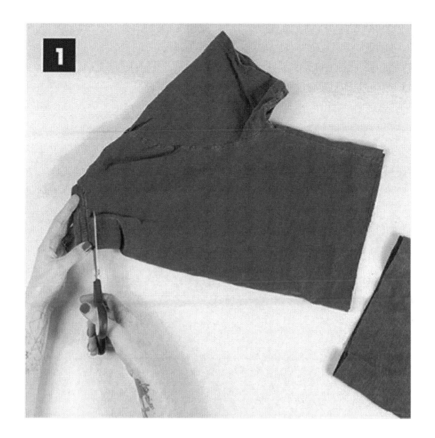

STEP 2

Using whichever colour yarn you choose to make the top stripe, thread the needle and work back stitches approximately 1cm ($\frac{1}{2}$in) in from the top cut edge of the neck. Join in same colour yarn with 1ch, then crochet 1 to 2dc around each stitch. You may find that you need a mixture of both depending on how wide your back stitch is.

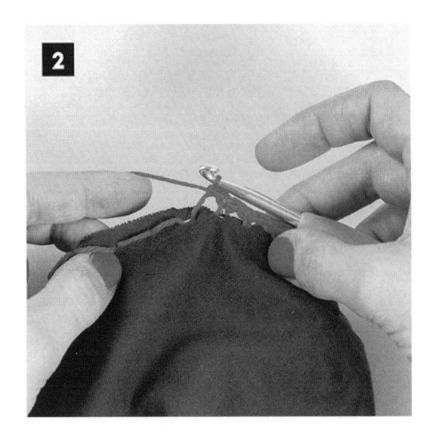

STEP 3

To make the scallop edge work: ch1 (does not count as st), (dc, skip 1 st, [tr, ch1, tr, ch1, tr] in next st, skip 1 st) all around the neck, ss in first dc. Fasten off.

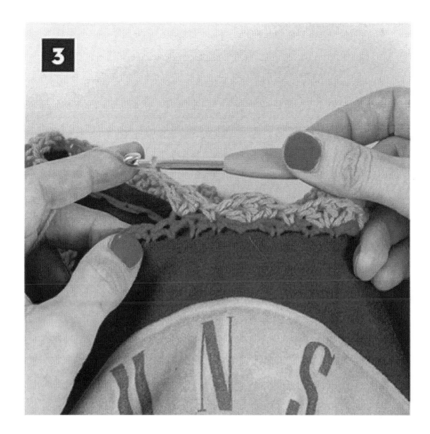

STEP 4
Repeat step 2 around the bottom edge of the tee and then work 4 rows of dc in colours of your choice.

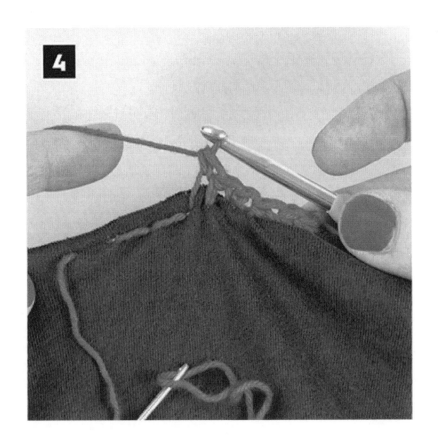

CUSTOM SLEEVE STRIPES

This bit of crochet hacking came about because I am quite a tall lady (nearly 5ft 10in) and most store bought sweatshirts just don't fit my long arms. Let's face it, not many of us are made to fit in-store bought clothes! Adding in a few rows of crochet has made them just the right length. This hack isn't just for sleeves that are too short, you could cut a section out and make them shorter if you prefer, or not reattach them at all and have a slouchy tee instead.

MATERIALS

- Jersey sweatshirt
- 4mm crochet hook
- Large eye embroidery needle
- Sharp scissors

- Aran (Worsted) weight yarn in five colours

You don't need a lot of yarn for this, I used a mix of Aran in acrylic and cotton. Raid your stash and find some colours that make you happy.

It is important that your tension is not too tight or too loose - add or subtract dc's to the running stitches to make it even.

STITCHES

CROCHET
dc – UK double (US single) crochet
tr – UK treble (US double) crochet
ch – chain
ss – slip stitch
st(s) – stitch(es)

SEWING
Back stitch

HOW TO

STEP 1
To cut the sleeves, fold the sweater so that the sleeves are lined up on top of each other and cut at the desired height.

STEP 2

Using whichever colour yarn you choose to make the top stripe, thread the needle and work back stitches approximately 1cm ($^{1}/_{2}$in) in from the top cut edge of the sleeve. Join in same colour yarn with 1ch then crochet 1 to 2dc around each stitch. You may find that you need a mixture of both depending on how wide your back stitch is.

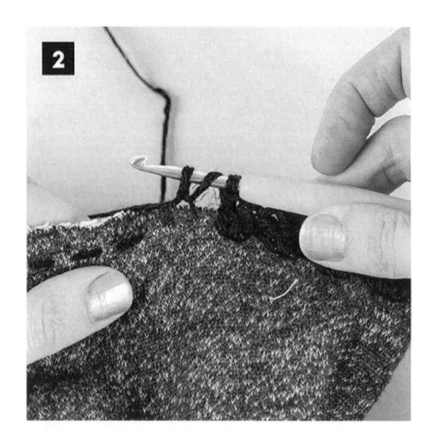

STEP 3
Using the rest of your yarns, work a round of dc in each colour, ss at the end of each round and fasten off.

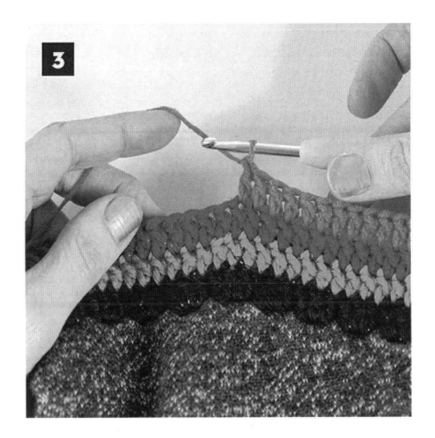

STEP 4
Reattach the bottom of the sleeve using a back stitch in a matching yarn.

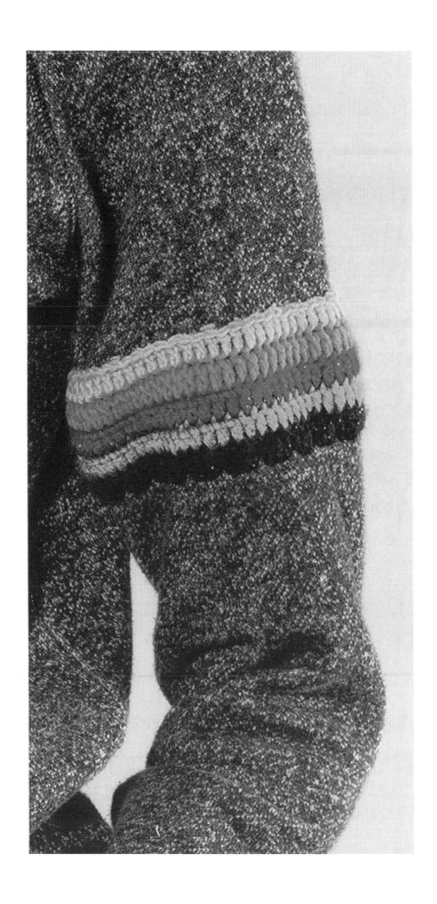

FAIRISLE STYLE CUFFS

This is one of my very first bits of crochet hacking, and like all the rest it came about through necessity. This jersey top is very old but very soft and one of my faves for wearing as an under layer but it only has three-quarter length sleeves. Last winter we were out having a family walk and those shorter sleeves were just leaving me all chilly around the edges, so when I got home, I had an experiment with a needle, some yarn and a crochet hook and added some new yarny cuffs. I could take them off again when I want the sleeves shorter and just use the cuffs as wrist warmers, but so far they're more fun this way!

MATERIALS

- Jersey t-shirt with three-quarter length sleeves
- 4mm crochet hook
- Large eye embroidery needle

- Sharp scissors
- DK (Light Worsted) or Aran (Worsted) weight yarn in various colours

You don't need a lot of yarn for this, I used a mix of DK and Aran in acrylic and cotton. Raid your stash and find some colours that make you happy.

STITCHES

CROCHET
dc – UK double (US single) crochet
exdc – UK extended double (US extended single) crochet
htr – UK half treble (US half double) crochet
ch – chain
ch sp – chain space
ss – slip stitch
st(s) – stitch(es)

SEWING
Back stitch

HOW TO

This fairisle style is made by working chains and dc's in one row, and then working into the chain space in the next row. It uses an extended double crochet which has the movement of a treble but the shorter length of a double.

The ribbing is made by working into the 'hump' part of a half treble stitch, so work an htr (hdc) and then roll it forward a little, the extra stitch you see is the back hump. Keep your tension correct by adding or subtracting dc's in the running stitches to keep the crochet flat.

STEP 1
Thread the needle with whichever yarn you would like to use first and work a few back stitches at approximately 1cm ($^1/_2$in) in from the edge of the sleeve. Join in same colour yarn with 1ch, then crochet 1

to 2dc around each stitch. You may find that you need a mixture of both depending on how wide your back stitch is. Keep going until you have reached the end.

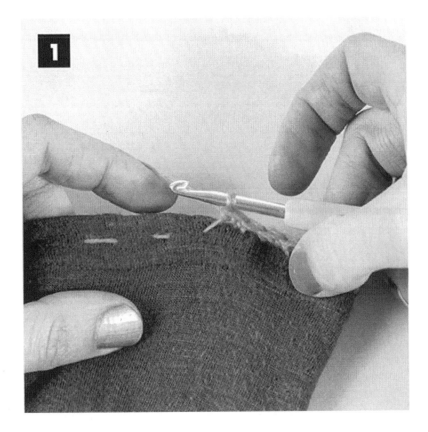

STEP 2
Round 1: ch1, exdc in each st and ss to join at end.
Rounds 21–36: ch1, exdc in each ch sp and ss to join at end.
Follow the grid pattern or make your own.

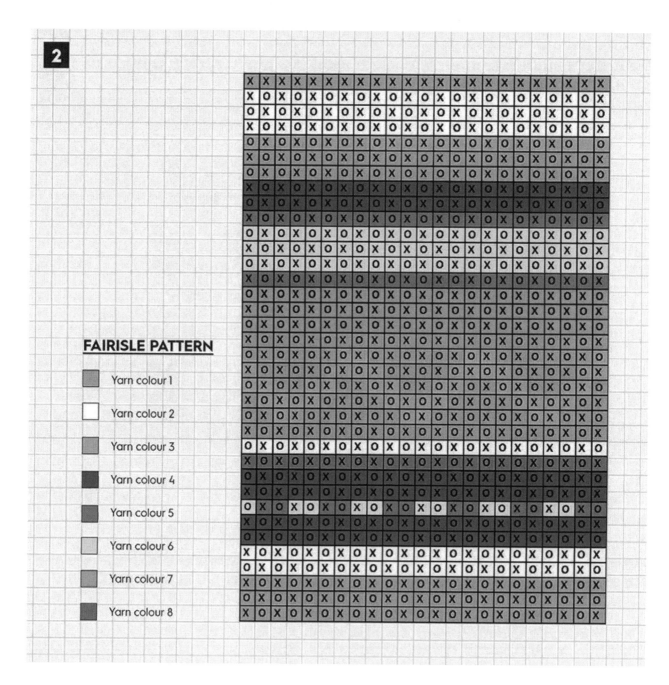

FAIRISLE PATTERN

- Yarn colour 1
- Yarn colour 2
- Yarn colour 3
- Yarn colour 4
- Yarn colour 5
- Yarn colour 6
- Yarn colour 7
- Yarn colour 8

STEP 3

RIB (WORKED SIDEWAYS)

Ch10.
Row 1: htr in 3rd ch from hook, htr in each st to end, turn.
Row 2: ch1 (does not count as st), htr in back hump of each st, turn.
Row 3: ch1 (does not count as st), htr in front loop of each st, turn.
Repeat rows 2 to 3 until the ribbed piece fits around the bottom of the fairisle cuff.

Whip stitch the ribbed piece to the end of the cuff and finish off with a contrasting row of dc around the ribbed edge.

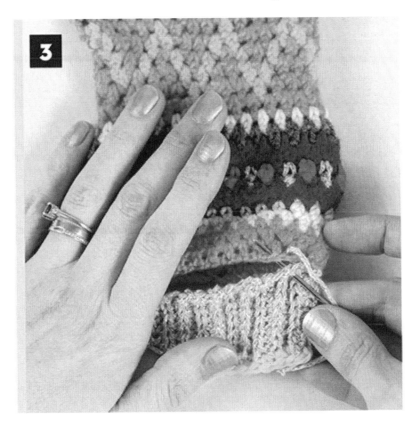

EEZYPEEZY ZIPPER JACKET

The idea of putting a zip in something can be terrifying for the uninitiated, but don't be scared. This zip is sewn in with a basic running stitch, by hand. No zipper feet to contend with, no faffing and fiddling, just a bit of pinning and sewing. If you don't feel like tackling it, don't, the world isn't going to end and you can add buttons or just leave it open if you prefer.

MATERIALS

- Sweatshirt
- 5mm crochet hook
- Large eye embroidery needle
- Sharp scissors

- Zip – suitable size for sweater
- Needle and thread
- Washable pen (if pockets required)
- Pins (if pockets required)
- DK (Light Worsted) or Aran (Worsted) weight yarn in five colours

I used a mix of DK and Aran yarn from my stash but you can use any yarn you like.

STITCHES

CROCHET
dc – UK double (US single) crochet
exdc – UK extended double (US extended single) crochet
ch – chain
ss – slip stitch
st(s) – stitch(es)

SEWING
Running stitch

HOW TO

STEP 1
Fold the sweatshirt in half and cut off the bottom so that it sits at waist height, then cut up the middle to make it into a jacket.

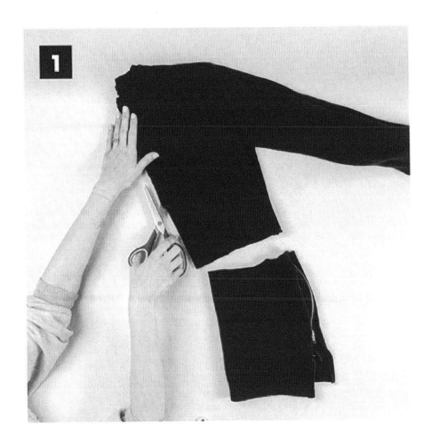

STEP 2

Using the embroidery needle and some yarn work a running stitch along the cut edge and around the bottom of the cardigan. Join in same colour yarn with 1ch and work 1 to 2dc in each stitch. The width of the running stitch will determine how many dc's you'll need to use.

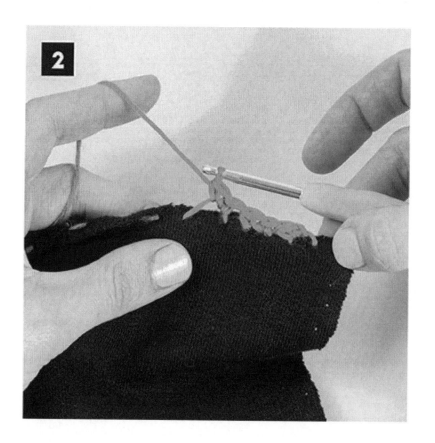

STEP 3
Round 1: using a different coloured yarn, ch1, dc in each st to end with [dc, ch2, dc] in each corner. Fasten off.

Rows 2–7: using a different colour yarn for each 2 rows and working along the bottom of the jacket **only**, ch2, exdc to end, turn.

Round 8: join a different colour yarn, ch1, dc in each st along the bottom and around the edges with [dc, ch2, dc] in each corner. Fasten off and weave in all ends.

3

STEP 4

To add the zip, hold or pin in place on the left side and use a running stitch to sew into place. Line up the right side and use a running stitch to sew into place. It is actually that easy!

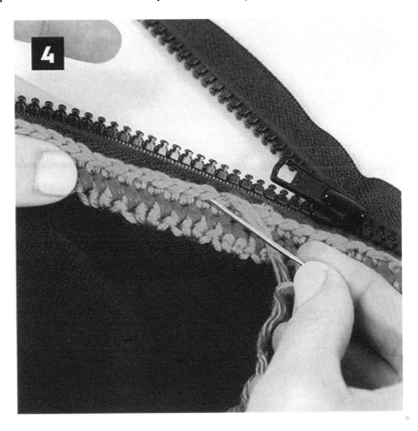

STEP 5

Go CRAZY and create any design that you like to decorate the back of your jacket. Experiment with stitches, go mad with fabric paint, applique, adorn and embellish to your heart's content. There are no rules for this bit other than to enjoy yourself.

STEP 6

Now it's time for those pockets, pop the jacket on and make a mark using a washable pen where you want the pockets to sit. Making sure they are symmetrically placed, make a straight cut about the same width as your hand.

Use the width of your cut as the measurement for the width of your pocket lining. To make the pocket lining cut 2 rectangles for each pocket and sew them together around three sides leaving an open edge. You can do this by hand or with a sewing machine.

On the inside of the jacket, pin and tack the pocket in place and sew one open edge to the top of the straight cut and the other to the bottom. This can be a bit fiddly, but once you have crocheted a new edge no one will see a thing!

Repeat steps 2 to 3 to make a new edge for the pocket with as many rows of crochet as you require then sew the edges of the crochet in place.

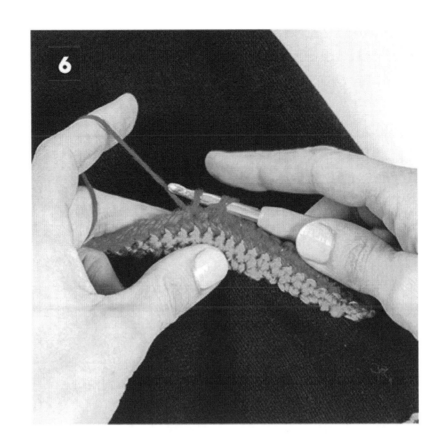

SLOUCHY COUCH CARDIGAN

There are so many possibilities when it comes to remaking a man's tee. This one was a basic long sleeve t-shirt that has been transformed with a simple slice up the middle and a bit of chopping around the neckline. Adding crochet pastel hues as a new edging makes it just right for springtime or bedtime.

MATERIALS

- T-shirt
- 5mm crochet hook
- Large eye embroidery needle
- Sharp scissors

- 6 small buttons
- Needle and thread
- Washable pen (if pockets required)
- Pins (if pockets required)
- Aran (Worsted) weight yarn in four colours

I used Aran acrylic from my stash but you can use any yarn you like.

STITCHES

CROCHET
dc – UK double (US single) crochet
exdc – UK extended double (US extended single) crochet
ch – chain
ch sp – chain space
ss – slip stitch
st(s) – stitch(es)

SEWING
Running stitch

HOW TO

STEP 1
Make a cut up the middle of the t-shirt, fanning out to create a 'V' shape as you get toward the neckline, and then cut around the neckline too. To make the cut symmetrical, cut one side first and then fold it over and use it as a template for the other side.

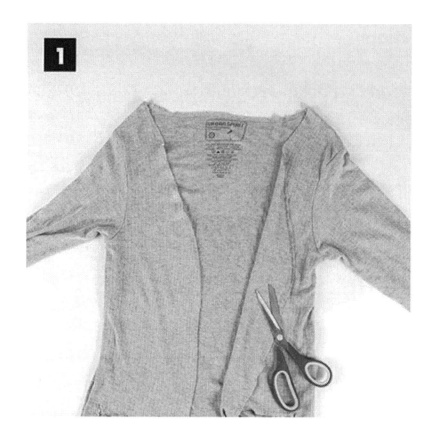

STEP 2

Using the embroidery needle and some yarn work a running stitch along the cut edge and around the bottom of the cardigan. Join in same colour yarn with 1ch and work a dc in a stitch on one side of the fabric and then work a dc in the stitch on the other side of the fabric. This prevents the jersey from curling one way or the other. Continue all around the edges. At the corners work [dc, ch2, dc], and ss in first dc to join at the end.

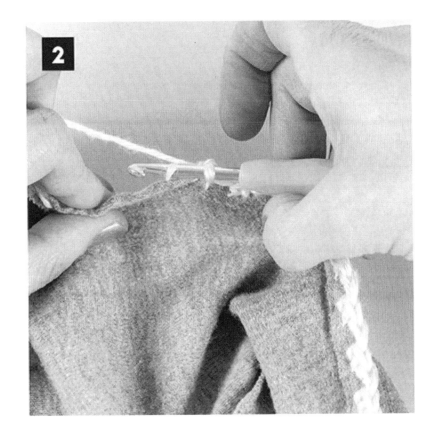

STEP 3

Row 1: using the same coloured yarn, ch1 (does not count as st), dc in each st to end with [dc, ch2, dc] in each corner ch sp and ss in first dc to join at end.

Rows 2–3: using a different colour yarn, ch2 (does not count as st), exdc in each st to end with [exdc, ch2, exdc] in each corner ch sp and ss in first exdc to join at end.

Row 4: using a different colour yarn, ch1 (does not count as st), dc in each st to end with [dc, ch2, dc] in each corner ch sp and ss in first dc to join at end.

Weave in all ends.

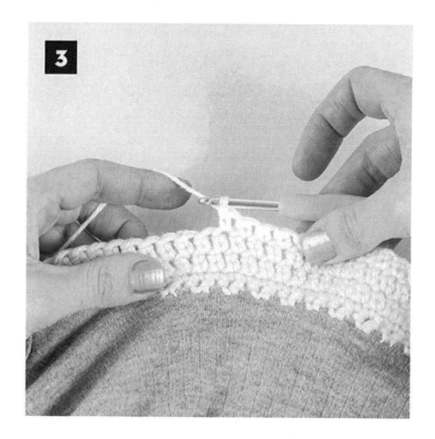

STEP 4

You can leave things there if you like, or if you want to add pockets, pop the cardigan on and make a mark using a washable pen where you want the pockets to sit. Making sure they are symmetrically placed, make a straight cut about the same width as your hand.

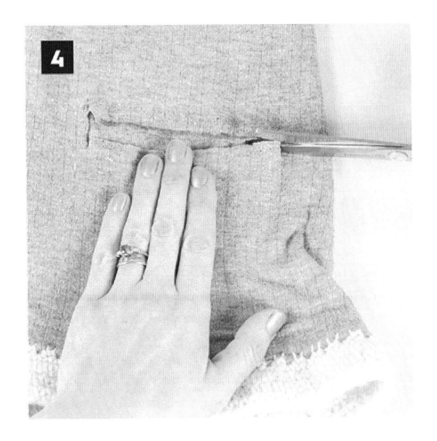

STEP 5

Use the width of your cut as the measurement for the width of your pocket lining. To make the pocket lining cut 2 rectangles for each pocket and sew them together around three sides leaving an open edge. You can do this by hand or with a sewing machine.

On the inside of the t-shirt, pin and tack the pocket in place and sew one open edge to the top of the straight cut and the other to the bottom. This can be a bit fiddly, but once you have crocheted a new edge no one will see a thing!

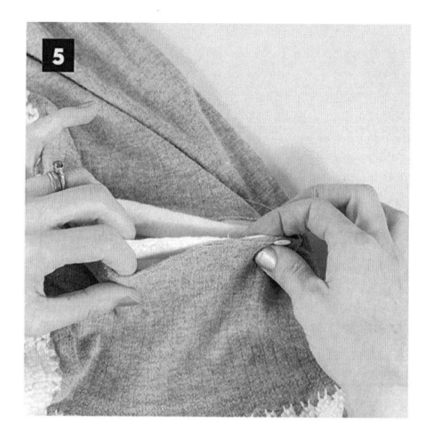

STEP 6
Repeat steps 2 to 3 to make a new edge for the pocket, sew the edges of the crochet in place.

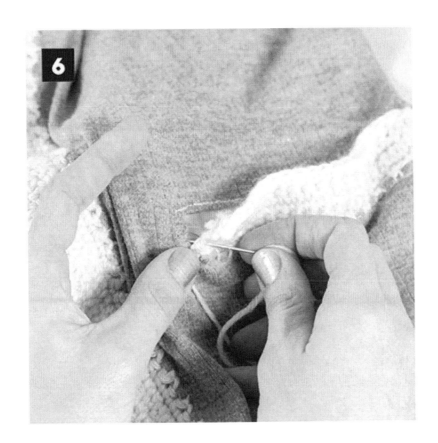

STEP 7

Sew on the buttons, you won't need to add buttonholes as you can use the spaces between the crochet stitches.

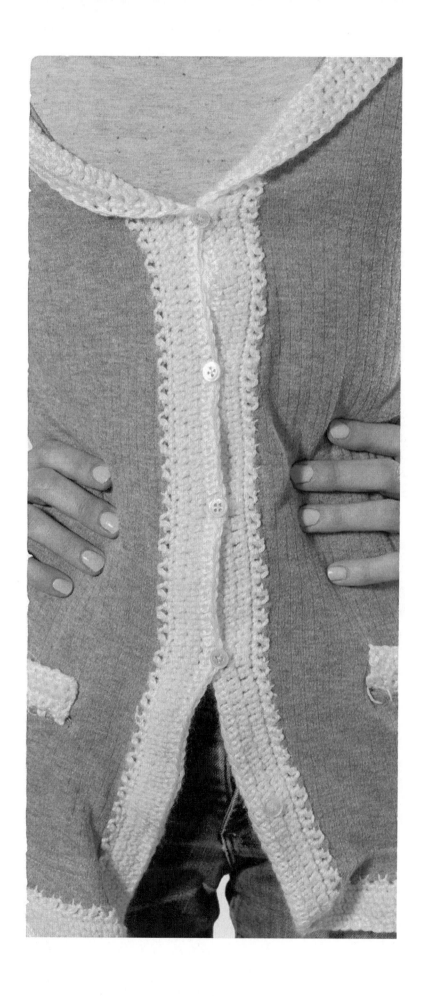

146

BIKINI
BIRD
DRESS BEACH

As a lady that can get a little self-conscious, I love the idea of being out in a bikini top but don't always want to show my tummy. This bit of crochet hacking uses an old tee to create an empire style beach dress, perfect for keeping cool but covering up.

MATERIALS

- Large t-shirt (wide enough to go over your hips)
- 4mm crochet hook
- Large eye embroidery needle

- Sharp scissors
- Needle and thread or a sewing machine if you have one
- DK (Light Worsted) weight cotton yarn in colours of your choice

I used Paintbox Simply Cotton in shades Blush Pink, Daffodil Yellow, Mustard Yellow, Bubble Gum, Lipstick, Slate and Washed Teal.

STITCHES

CROCHET
dc – UK double (US single) crochet
tr – UK treble (US double) crochet
ch – chain
ch sp – chain space
ss – slip stitch
st(s) – stitch(es)

SEWING
Back stitch
Running stitch

HOW TO

STEP 1
Fold the t-shirt in half lengthways and cut off the neckline; the fold helps keeps it symmetrical. Turn the t-shirt inside out, cut off the sleeves and sew up the holes following the line of the edge seams.

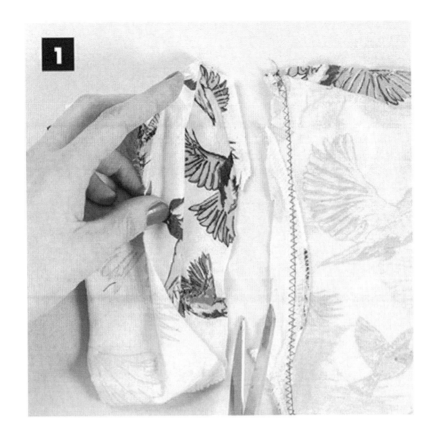

STEP 2

This bikini fits my 36B frame, to make the cups smaller finish the repeat at row 7, to make the cups larger continue repeating the pattern after row 8 until it's the desired size. To make the band larger or smaller work the starting chain to fit to your body.

BIKINI CUPS (MAKE 2)

Ch10.
Row 1: ch2 (does not count as st), tr in 3rd ch from hook, tr in next 8 ch, [2tr, ch1, 2tr] in end ch, tr in each st on other side of ch to end, turn. (22 sts and 1 ch)
Row 2–8: ch2 (does not count as st), tr in each st to ch sp, [2tr, ch1, 2ch] in ch sp, tr in each st to end, turn. (50 sts and 1 ch after row 8 – see note on sizing above). Fasten off once you are happy with the size.

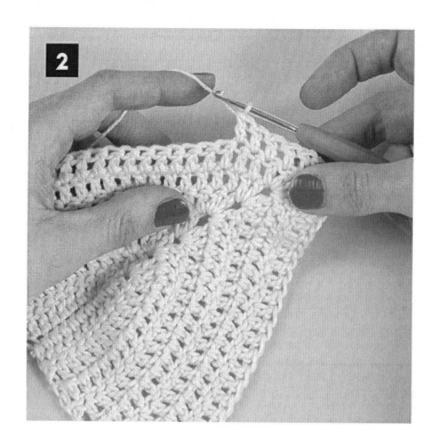

STEP 3

BIKINI BAND

Ch105, ss to first ch to make a loop. Adjust the number of ch if required so that the length fits around your body under the bust.
Rounds 1–7: ch1 (does not count as st), dc in each st, ss in first dc. Using the embroidery needle and matching yarn, attach the cups to the band at the desired distance apart. I left a gap of 3 sts between my cups. Work a row of dc around the edge of each cup starting at the bottom right of the right cup and finishing at the bottom left of the left cup.

STEP 4

Run a loose row of running stitches around the top edge of the t-shirt - this needs to be using one length of thread. Pull one end and gather up the fabric so that the top of the tee is the same size as the band of the bikini. This can take a bit of fiddling and faffing to make sure that the fabric is evenly distributed along the thread.

STEP 5
Sew the tee to the bikini band using back stitch or your sewing machine.

STEP 6

You can get as creative as you like for the straps, plait together lengths of coloured yarn, use strips of ribbon or crochet coloured rows. As long as the length of material is enough to go from the top of the cup to the edging at the back without being too loose or too tight. Try it on as you go to find out!

I chose to cut 50cm (20in) lengths of yarn, knot one end together and sew it into the cup. I then knotted each of the straps together in the middle of the back and sewed the ends into the edging.

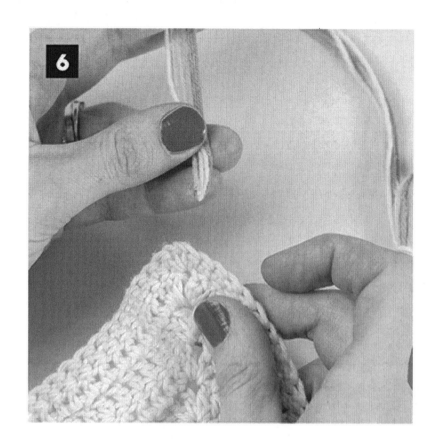

CROCHET IS A SUPER POWER

DON'T LET ANYONE TELL YOU OTHERWISE

WOOL
AND OTHER
FABRICS

It would be a bold undertaking to try and talk about *all* the other fabrics there are in the world. There are an awful lot, from chiffon to tweed, organza to felt, natural and man-made, each with its own unique qualities. In this chapter I have tried to share a variety of makes that will allow you to learn different techniques and give you a good introduction to working with almost any material.

"SECOND-HAND STORES ARE FULL OF ABANDONED KNITWEAR AND THINKING OF THEM AS MATERIAL RATHER THAN A

GARMENT CAN OPEN UP HUNDREDS OF CRAFTING POSSIBILITIES."

It was while browsing Pinterest, when researching for my MA, that I first came across an illustration of a jumper, marked out with where to cut to make a pair of mittens, a woolly hat and a scarf. I have often made a pair of leg warmers from hacked jumper sleeves and made the boys mittens from a felted jumper, but seeing the opportunities within one jumper, set out so clearly was a revelation.

Second-hand stores are full of abandoned knitwear and thinking of them as material rather than a garment can open up hundreds of crafting possibilities.

However, cutting into knitting is a terrifying proposition, but once you learn the secret to a bit of 'steeking', the terror is replaced with delight and you can take on almost anything.

Knitwear is also great for working into, popping your crochet hook around those already made stitches and making a new stitch on top is a brilliant way to reinvent something. If you can stick a hook in it, you can crochet it (if that isn't a saying then it really should be!) They are also ripe and ready for any sort of embellishment that takes your fancy. Making crochet elements to sew on, just snipping out bits of fabric and working a bit of applique magic, or having a go at a bit of freestyle embroidery are all ways to transform something plain and let you fall in love with it all over again. And when you've had enough, snip it all off and do something new.

This section of the book will also introduce you to techniques that allow you to work into rubber, foam and plastic. The 'throwaway' spa slipper transformation can be used on flipflops too, the IKEA bag upcycle techniques could be used on anything from a bag for life to a defunct inflatable, the possibilities are literally endless. As with all the other patterns in this book, these patterns should be thought of more as guidelines. We all make things differently, stitch tension will vary from person to person, sizing and shaping will be down to your own size and shape, so use these techniques as tools and enjoy yourself with your experimentation. Nothing that you do will be 'wrong', you will just have learned how not to do something.

HOW TO WORK CROCHET INTO WOOL AND OTHER FABRICS

There is a technique called 'steeking' where designers specifically add an extra few stitches in a knitted garment so that they can cut into it and hem it later. This technique can be used on any knitted garment, whether it was designed that way or not, and it involves threading a length of yarn through the stitches so that they don't all unravel once you have made a cut. Alternatively you can cut and hem just as you would any other fabric.

TOOLS

FOR KNITWEAR
A good, sharp pair of scissors, yarn and an embroidery needle are essential for working into knitwear. It's also a good idea to have some yarn pins to hand especially for a project like adding a new yoke, as they have a larger head than regular fabric pins and will allow you to line things up just right before you get sewing.

FOR PLASTIC
You can use any hole making tools that you like with plastic.

FOR RUBBER, FOAM AND THICK MATERIALS
Use a bodkin or bradawl to make the first hole, then widen the hole with a knitting needle thicker than the crochet hook you will use. I use a 4mm needle. For the crochet hook I use a 3mm or 3.5mm hook, even when using Aran weight yarn.

TECHNIQUES

STEEKING KNITWEAR

You can either cut into the knitting first, leaving a good 5cm (2in) of seam allowance if possible and then pick up all the stitches with a needle and length of yarn OR work the sewing first and then cut leaving a 1cm ($^1/_2$in) allowance from the sewn in yarn. Either way is fine, I tend to cut first and sew later but it is less risky to do it the other way around.

STEP 1
Thread the needle but don't tie a knot in the end, you just need to ensure that you have a long enough length of yarn to have a long 'tail' at the end. Insert the needle into a loop of the knitted stitches, then work a running stitch, picking up each loop of each knitted stitch on your needle. Gently draw through the yarn leaving a good length tail.

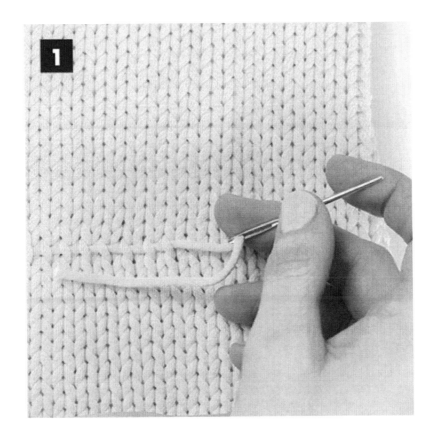

STEP 2

Repeat the last step until you have reached the end. You can now grab a crochet hook, insert it into the first knit loop and start crocheting, picking up each steeked stitch as you go. You will need to select a matching yarn weight if possible and a suitable size hook for this method.

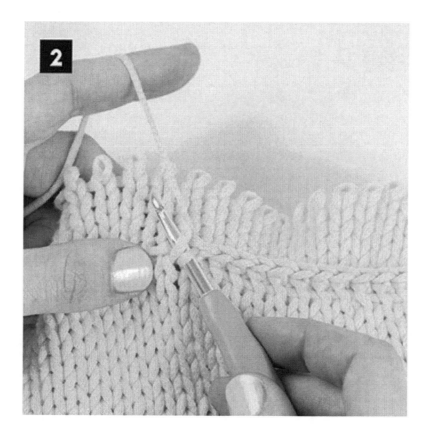

STEP 3

Once you have all your crochet in place you can pull out all the spare threads from the knitting and remove them.

HEMMING KNITWEAR

STEP 1

Cut the knitted garment leaving a 2 to 3cm ($^3/_4$ to $1^1/_4$in) seam allowance along the area where you want to hem.

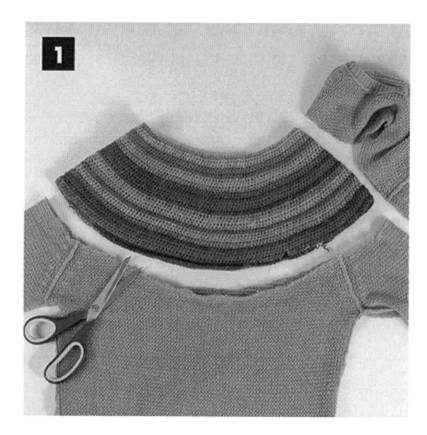

STEP 2

Pin the new yoke in place. Using a yarn needle and matching yarn hand sew the new piece of crochet in place using back stitches.

STEP 3

On the back of the work hand sew another row around the cut edge of the knit. This doesn't have to be beautiful, it just has to hold all the loose edges to make sure they don't fray.

Did you know: More than 15 million tons of used textile waste is generated every year. Instead of it becoming waste we can turn it into something new!

WORKING INTO RUBBER, FOAM AND THICK MATERIALS

Working into thick materials is a bit more physically demanding as it relies entirely on making holes in things, but although it's a bit more effort the results can be transformational. This is also where a bradawl or bodkin and a knitting needle will become your best friends. This technique is not the definitive way to do this, it's just a way I've found that works, there may be much better, more efficient ways of doing it, so don't be afraid to experiment.

STEP 1
Work a sample bit of crochet using your final hook size. Measure out the space of the holes using the crochet sample as a template. Mark every other stitch or every third stitch depending on the pattern.

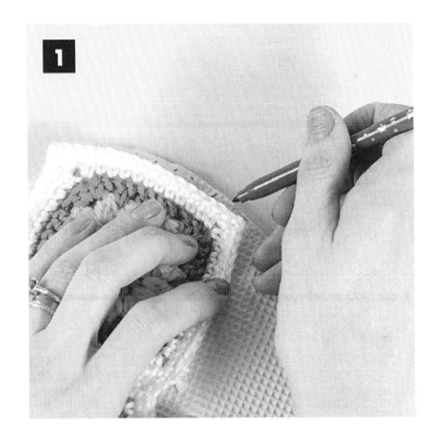

STEP 2
Make holes first with the bodkin, then with the knitting needle to widen them.

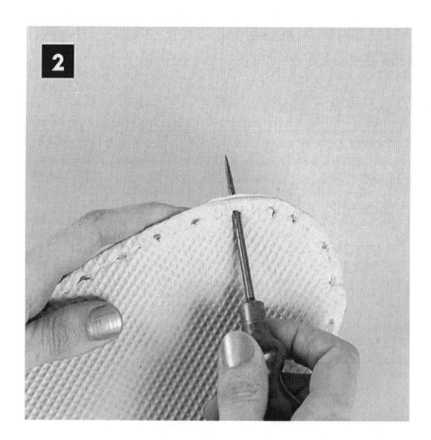

STEP 3

Insert crochet hook into a hole, draw a up a loop, ch1 (this does not count as a st) and continue to crochet in each hole following the pattern.

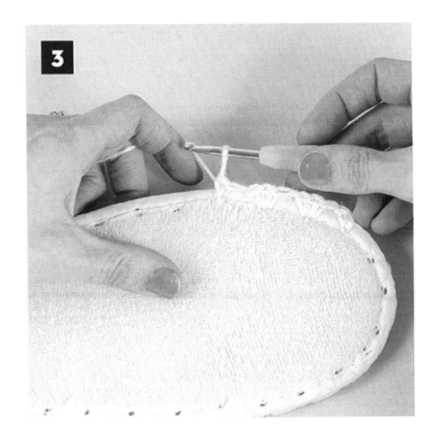

WORKING INTO PLASTIC

Each plastic will behave a little differently so it's always worth doing a test first. The main thing is that it will usually need to be folded over and 'hemmed' so that you work through two layers at a time.

STEP 1
Cut to the right shape leaving a 1.5cm ($^1/_2$in) seam allowance. Fold hem and make holes through both layers.

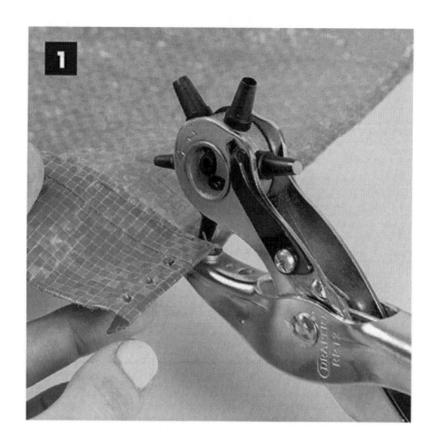

STEP 2
Insert hook and crochet away!

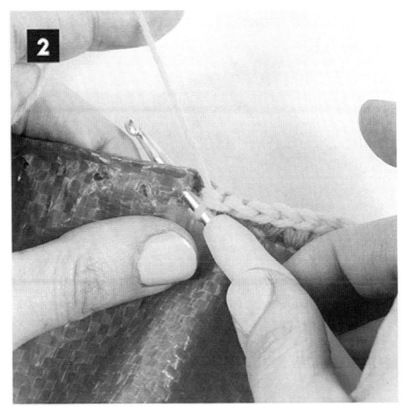

Did you know: A plastic bag takes up to 500 years to decay in landfill. IKEA has been looking at the issue of how to reduce the environmental impact of its bags for a number of years. The project in this book is a great start!

ALL THE FUN
AND NONE OF THE EFFORT
JUMPER

I love a fancy Fairilse yoke jumper but have never made one because I just don't have the patience for it. Making just a yoke is the ideal solution, it's given a second life to a rescued, acrylic mix jumper; allows me to enjoy the colours and creation of using a variegated yarn and is relatively quick to whip up, all the fun and none of the effort!

MATERIALS

- Knitted jumper
- 4mm crochet hook
- Large eye embroidery needle
- Sharp scissors

- Washable pen
- DK (Light Worsted) variegated yarn

I used King Cole Riot DK in 'Carnival' as it had been donated to my stash by a friend, but you can use any yarn you like. Feel free to mix up your own stripes with lots of different yarns, just make sure they're the same weight.

STITCHES

CROCHET
dc – UK double (US single) crochet
tr – UK treble (US double) crochet
ch – chain
ss – slip stitch
st(s) – stitch(es)

SEWING
Back stitch

HOW TO

STEP 1
To crochet the yoke make a starting ch and ss to the first ch to make a loop. Pop it over your head and see how it sits, this will be the neckline. Make this whatever size works for you. I worked 126 ch as I like quite a wide neck.

Round 1: ch1 (does not count as st), dc in each st to the end, ss in first dc to join.

Rounds 2–18: ch2 (does not count as st), tr in each st, but work 2tr in each st at 4 random points in each round to make the increases, ss in first tr to join. Spread the increases apart to allow the yoke to grow in an even shape. Placing them at random points will prevent 'straight' edges being formed.

If you'd like your yoke to be longer continue as in rounds 2 to 18. Keep checking the size and shape of your yoke by lying it over your jumper, you might find that you want to reduce or increase the number of treble increases that you work.

STEP 2

Turn the jumper inside out and lay the yoke on top to check it is the right size. Draw around the yoke with a washable pen. Add a few cm to create a seam allowance and cut.

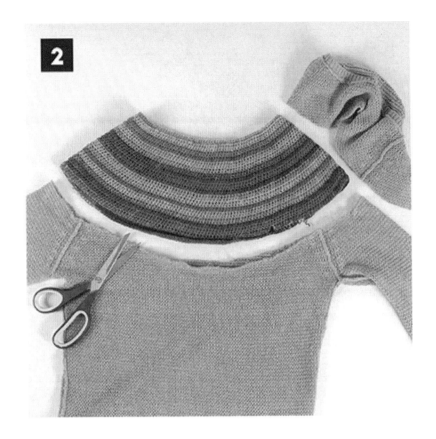

STEP 3
Turn the jumper the right way out and carefully pin the yoke in place. Make sure you don't stretch or fray the cut edge of the jumper. Back stitch the yoke in place.

STEP 4

You won't be able to steek this beforehand as the shape doesn't follow the weave of the knit, but once you've sewn everything into place you can secure the loose edge with some sewing stitches and get rid of the loose ends.

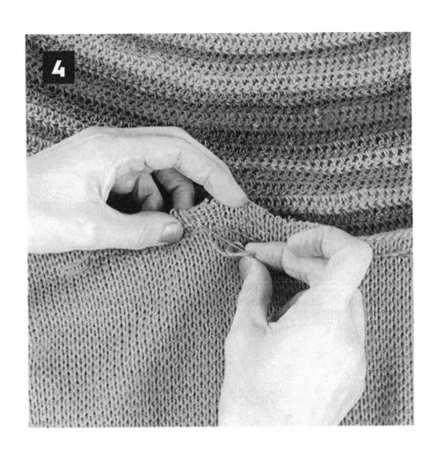

IKEA
BAG
HACK

Most of us will have been to IKEA at some point and most of us will have bought so much stuff that we needed an enormous plastic/canvas bag to carry all our treasured Scandi homewares home. We used our bags for all sorts of things, until we went one step too far by using them to carry a million tonnes of reclaimed ceramic tiles. Rather than throwing away the torn and dusty remains, I gave one a clean and thought it would be quite cool to turn it into an everyday, tote style bag. The technique for crocheting into this sort of fabric would work just as well with any tough plastic like old inflatables.

MATERIALS

- Old IKEA bag
- 4mm crochet hook
- Hole making tool

- Sharp scissors
- Aran (Worsted) weight yarn

I used an Aran weight cotton for this, used with a 4mm hook it makes quite a dense, sturdy material and the cotton will not stretch.

STITCHES

CROCHET
dc – UK double (US single) crochet
tr – UK treble (US double) crochet
ch – chain
ss – slip stitch
st(s) – stitch(es)

SEWING
Whip stitch

HOW TO

STEP 1
Cut the bag into a front and back piece for the new size bag that you would like to make, mine is approximately 30x40cm (12x16in) leaving a 1.5cm ($\frac{1}{2}$in) seam allowance.

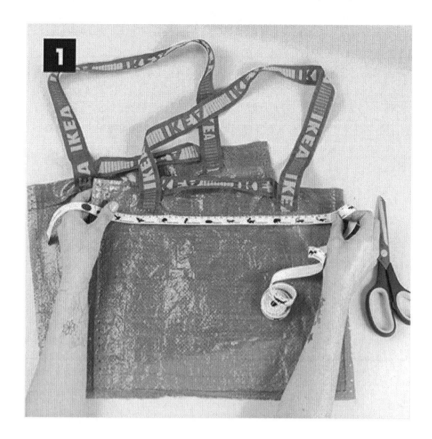

STEP 2
On each piece fold the seam allowance over and make holes through both layers along the sides and bottom edge.

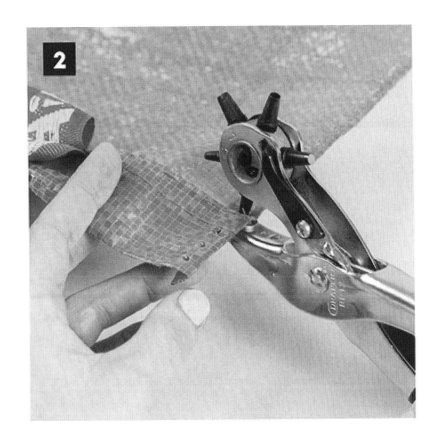

STEP 3

With front side of one piece facing, join yarn with 1ch and work 2dc in each hole around the sides and the bottom with [2dc, ch2, 2dc] in each corner hole, turn.

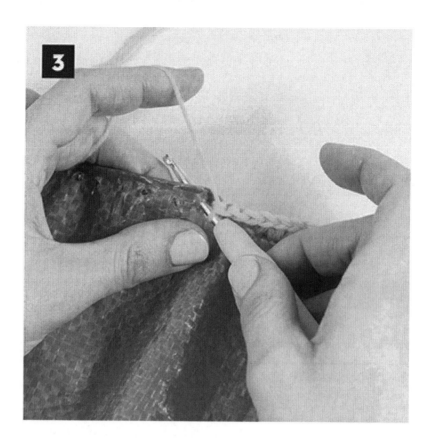

STEP 4
Row 1: ch2 (does not count as st), working in the back loop only, tr in each st to the end, turn.
Row 2: ch2 (does not count as st), tr in each st to the end, turn.
Row 3: ch2 (does not count as st), tr in each st to the end, fasten off.
Repeat steps 3 and 4 for the second piece.

STEP 5
Whip stitch front and back pieces together.

SUMMER BREEZE WRAP

I whipped this little kimono style jacket up to take on holiday but I'm so in love with it I think it's going to become a permanent wardrobe fixture, probably as a summer dressing gown! I love the long, sweeping tassels, but you could make them any length you like or even leave them off altogether.

MATERIALS

- Scarf
- 4mm crochet hook
- Large eye embroidery needle
- Sharp scissors

- Needle and thread or a sewing machine if you have one
- Any DK (Light Worsetd) cotton yarn in the colour of choice, the longer the fringing, the more yarn you will use.

I used a rectangular 90x180cm (35$^{1}/_{2}$x71in) scarf, but I have also used 135x135cm (53x53in) scarves to make these wraps.

STITCHES

CROCHET
dc – UK double (US single) crochet
tr – UK treble (US double) crochet
ch - chain
ss – slip stitch
st(s) – stitch(es)

SEWING
Running stitch

HOW TO

STEP 1
Fold the scarf in half and in half again. Cut along the centre fold of one edge, through just one layer, and cut a gentle curve out of the corner along the open edge through all the layers.

STEP 2

Open out the scarf and sew the curved edges together to make the underarm sleeve seams. You can hem the middle cut as well if you like; just fold it over a little, fold it over again and stitch in place using a needle and thread or a sewing machine.

STEP 3

To add the crochet, fold over the bottom edge and work a row of running stitches with a yarn needle and some cotton thread. Join in same colour yarn with 1ch and after every 10 stitches or so crochet 2dc into each stitch using the crochet hook and cotton yarn. This is row 1.

The reason for crocheting as you go is to stop the fabric from puckering if you've made your stitches too tight. When you run out of sewing yarn just fasten off, thread a new length and carry on until you reach the end.

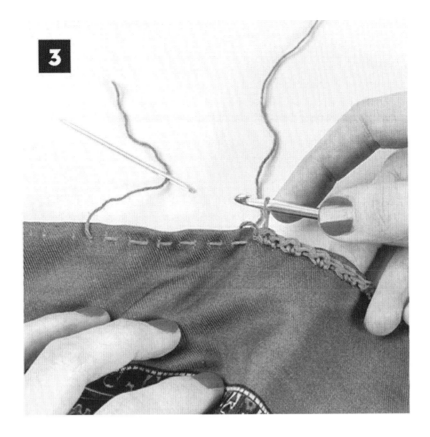

STEP 4

Now simply crochet into the sts you made in row 1, working as many rows of crochet as you like. I worked one row of tr and one row of dc.

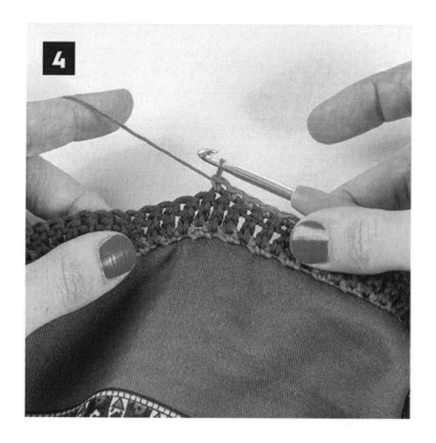

STEP 5

To make the fringing cut 60cm (24in) lengths of yarn, fold in half, use the crochet hook to pull the loop through a stitch, hook the long tail and pull it through the loop.

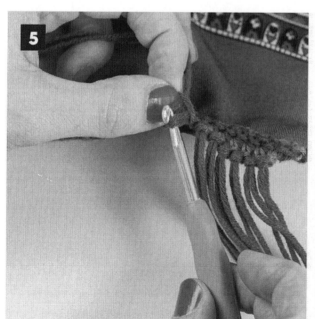

GO *FASTER*
RETRO
LEGWARMERS

As a wearer of skinny jeans with a turn up, I am also a massive fan of 80's retro so in the winter legwarmers are an intrinsic part of my wardrobe. After remaking a knitted jumper into a summery tee, I had some sleeves left over that were just perfect for reusing.

MATERIALS

- Chunky knitted jumper
- Suitable size crochet hook for yarn
- Large eye embroidery needle
- Sharp scissors
- Yarn in 2 colours

Try to find a yarn that matches the thickness of the existing knit as this will give a tidier finish.

STITCHES

CROCHET
dc – UK double (US single) crochet
ch – chain
ss – slip stitch
st(s) – stitch(es)

SEWING
Embroidery

HOW TO

STEP 1
Cut the sleeves off to the desired length. Take a length of yarn and 'steek' the stitches a few cm from the cut edge (see Techniques at start of this chapter). Don't knot the end, just leave a nice long tail. This thread will be removed after you have finished crocheting.

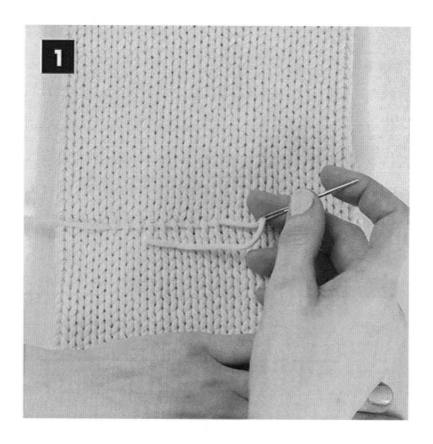

STEP 2

Join in same colour yarn with 1ch and work a round of dc directly into the steeked knit stitches.

Round 2: change colour, ch1 (does not count as st) and dc in each st to end, ss in first dc and fasten off.

Remove the steek thread from step 1.

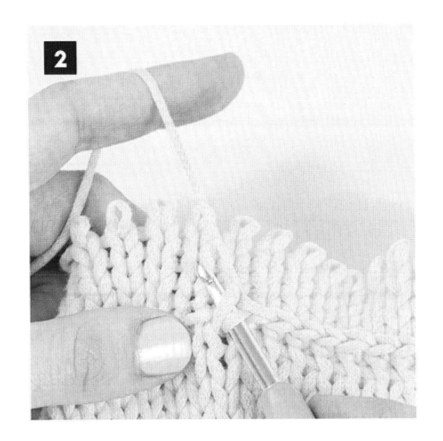

STEP 3
Trim the edge of the knit back to the steeked line.

STEP 4

Using the yarn needle hand stitch some 'go faster' stripes down the outer edge of each legwarmer. Following the 'V' pattern made by the knit stitches will give a sneaky knitted colourwork look.

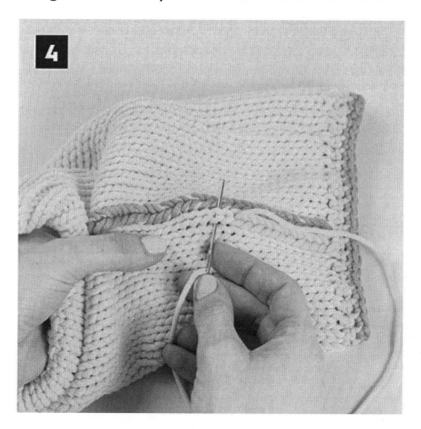

A JUMPER
IS FOR LIFE
NOT JUST FOR
CHRISTMAS

While I can't take credit for the name of this make, I can completely get behind the message of it. I love Christmas, I love dressing up and I love getting into the spirit of any season, but I don't love things that are sold as 'throw away'. Why buy something that only has a two-week shelf life when you can adapt something you already have? Adding embellishments and decorations to stuff that's already in your wardrobe is brilliant for so many reasons I'm not even going to write them down, but the best part is you can take them off again in the New Year and make something new for next Christmas. This jumper uses some classic crochet stars sewn on with a bit of yarn and a nifty bit of bobble making.

MATERIALS

- Knitted jumper
- 4mm crochet hook
- Large eye embroidery needle
- Sharp scissors

- Any yarn, I have used Aran (Worsted) acrylic.

You don't have to use a knitted jumper for this, you can use anything that you can get a hook in. This is a great project for using up ends of yarn and it doesn't just have to be for Christmas, you can embellish your jumper whenever you like!

STITCHES

CROCHET
dc – UK double (US single) crochet
tr – UK treble (US double) crochet
ch – chain
ch sp – chain space
ss – slip stitch
st(s) – stitch(es)

SEWING
Running stitch

HOW TO

BOBBLES

STEP 1
Insert the hook under a stitch in the jumper, yarn over and draw up a loop of yarn. Work a popcorn stitch: ch3, *yarn over, insert hook into the same stitch, yarn over and draw up a loop, yarn over and pull through 2 loops leaving 2 loops on the hook, repeat from * 4 more times so that you have a total of 6 loops on the hook. Yarn over and pull through all 6 loops.

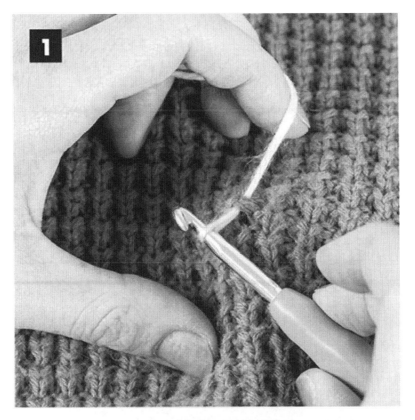

STEP 2

Insert the hook into a stitch a little above where you started, yarn over, draw up a loop and ss. Fasten off and pull threads through to the back and tie off. Make as many bobbles as you like.

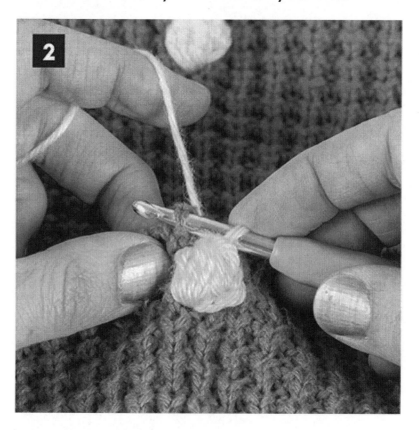

STARS

STEP 3
Ch3, ss to beginning ch to make a loop.
Round 1: in the loop work ch3 (counts as tr), 2tr, (ch2, 3tr) 4 times, ch2, ss to top of ch3, fasten off.
Round 2: rejoin yarn in a ch sp, [ch3, 2tr, ch3, 3tr] in the ch sp, ss into middle st of 3tr in previous row, *[3tr, ch3, 3tr] in next ch sp, ss into middle st of 3tr in previous row, repeat from * to end, ss in top of ch3 to finish. Fasten off.

STEP 4
Use a little matching yarn and a yarn needle to sew in place.

MAGIC GRANNY SLIPPERS

Some friends and I trotted off for a spa day recently and were given some simple little slippers to wear while we were doing our child-free relaxing. While getting changed to go home, I was told that the slippers just get thrown away when they're finished with. Naturally, I couldn't be having that, so I popped them in my bag and brought them home. With a few snips of the scissors, some holes stabbed in the edges and the magic of a couple of granny squares later a pair of throw-away slippers have become a pair of forever slippers.

MATERIALS

- Pair of 'disposable' slippers or flip-flops
- 4mm crochet hook
- Bodkin or sharp knitting needle
- Large eye embroidery needle

- Sharp scissors
- Aran (Worsted) weight yarn in 5 colours (yarns A-E).

I used an Aran weight acrylic yarn with a 4mm hook as it makes quite a dense, sturdy material.

STITCHES

CROCHET
dc – UK double (US single) crochet
tr – UK treble (US double) crochet
tr2tog or tr3tog – work 2 or 3 UK trebles (US doubles) together in same sp or st to make one stitch
ch – chain
ch sp – chain space
ss – slip stitch
st(s) – stitch(es)

SEWING
Whip stitch

HOW TO

These squares fit a shoe base of UK women's size 6–7 (US 8$\frac{1}{2}$–9$\frac{1}{2}$). If you have smaller or larger size soles, just make sure that the square is a little wider than the shoe base when finished. You can change the size by using lighter or heavier weight yarn and a smaller or larger hook or working less or more rounds of the square.

STEP 1
Cut off the slipper upper or the plastic thong from a flip flop (the bit that holds the shoe to your foot) and make holes around the edge of the shoe sole approximately 2cm (1in) apart. Join yarn A with 1ch and crochet 3dc in each hole, ss in first dc and fasten off.
Round 1: using yarn B, ch1 (does not count as st) dc in each st to the end, ss in first dc, fasten off.
Rounds 2–4: repeat round 1 using yarns C, then D, then A.

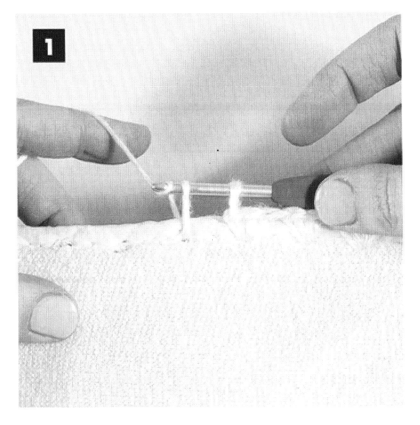

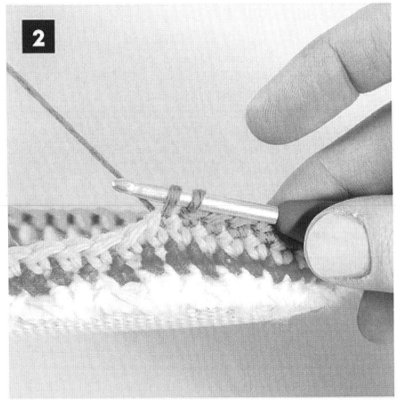

STEP 3

GRANNY SQUARES (MAKE 2)

Using yarn E, ch3, ss in the first ch to make a loop.
Round 1: ch2 (counts as dc), 5dc in the loop, ss to top of ch2, fasten off. (6 dc)
Round 2: join yarn B in any st, ch4 (counts as tr and ch2), tr in same st, ch2, [tr, ch2, tr, ch2] in each st to the end, ss to second ch in ch4, fasten off. (12 tr, 12 ch sp)
Round 3: join yarn C in any ch sp, ch2 (counts as first part of tr3tog), [tr2tog, ch3, tr3tog] in same ch sp, *(tr3tog in next ch sp) twice, [tr3tog, ch3, tr3tog] in next ch sp, rep from * twice more, tr3tog in each of last 2 ch sp, ss to top of ch2, fasten off. (16 tr3tog, 4 ch sp)
Round 4: join yarn D in any ch sp, ch2 (counts as tr), [tr, ch2, 2tr] in same ch sp, *work 2tr in each gap between sts to the next ch sp, [2tr, ch2, 2tr] in ch sp, rep from * twice, work 2tr in each gap between sts to the end, ss to top of ch2, fasten off. (20 groups of 2tr, 4 ch sp)
Round 5: join yarn A in any ch sp, ch1, [dc, ch2, dc] in same ch sp, *dc in each st to next ch sp, [dc, ch2, dc] in ch sp, rep from * twice, dc in each st to end, ss in first dc. (48 dc, 4 ch sp)
Round 6: ss in ch sp, ch1, [dc, ch2, dc] in same ch sp, *dc in each st to next ch sp, [dc, ch2, dc] in ch sp, rep from * twice, dc in each st to end, ss in first dc, fasten off. (56 dc, 4 ch sp)

HALF GRANNY SQUARES (MAKE 4)

Using yarn E, ch3.
Row 1: 2dc in third ch from hook, first 2ch count as dc, turn, fasten off. (3 dc)
Row 2: join yarn B, ch2 (counts as tr), ch2, tr in same st, ch2, [tr, ch2, tr, ch2] in each st to the end, omitting last ch2, turn, fasten off. (6 tr, 5 ch sp)
Row 3: join yarn C, ch2 (counts as first part of tr3tog), tr2tog in same st, (tr3tog in next ch sp) twice, [tr3tog, ch3, tr3tog] in next ch sp, tr3tog in each of last 2 ch sp, tr3tog in last st, turn, fasten off. (8 tr3tog, 1 ch sp)
Row 4: join yarn D, ch2 (counts as tr), 2tr in each gap between sts to the next ch sp, [2tr, ch2, 2tr] in ch sp, 2tr in each gap between sts to the end, tr in last st, turn, fasten off. (8 groups of 2tr, 2 single tr, 1 ch sp)
Row 5: join yarn A, ch1 (does not count as st), dc in each st to ch sp, [dc, ch2, dc] in ch sp, dc in each st to end, turn. (20 dc, 1 ch sp)

Round 6: ch1 (does not count as st), dc in each st to ch sp, [dc, ch2, dc] in ch sp, dc in each st to end, continue along bottom of triangle by working 2dc around post of each row end st, ss to first st, fasten off. Whip stitch the square to the 2 triangles to make an upside down 'V' shape. This is the new slipper upper.

STEP 4

Line up the centre point of the square with the middle front of the sole and whip stitch the new upper to the sole.

GENERAL TECHNIQUES

HOW TO CROCHET

If you are new to crochet, hold the yarn however feels comfortable to you. There are ways you can hold it to maintain a certain tension but in the beginning it's best just to get a feel for working with the yarn. If you are right–handed, hold the hook in your right hand and the yarn in your left.

How to work each stitch is described in full below. To make things a bit more tricky the names for some stitches are different in the UK to the US. So that we are all on the same page here is a conversion chart.

UK STITCHES		US STITCHES	
ch	chain	ch	chain
ch sp	chain space	ch sp	chain space
ss	slip stitch	ss	slip stitch
dc	double crochet	sc	single crochet
exdc	extended double crochet	exsc	extended single crochet
2dc	double crochet increase	2sc	single crochet increase
dc2tog	double crochet 2 together	sc2tog	single crochet 2 together
htr	half treble crochet	hdc	half double crochet
tr	treble crochet	dc	double crochet
tr2tog	treble crochet 2 together	dc2tog	double crochet 2 together
tr3tog	treble crochet 3 together	dc3tog	double crochet 3 together

STITCHES

SLIP KNOT

This is the starting point for any crochet work. The simplest way to make a slip knot is to lay the yarn on a flat surface, cross the yarn over to make a loop **(1)**, pick the loop up and drop it over the tail end of the yarn to make a pretzel shape and then pull the tail yarn up through the loop **(2)**. Pull to tighten **(3)** and then slip on to the crochet hook **(4)**.

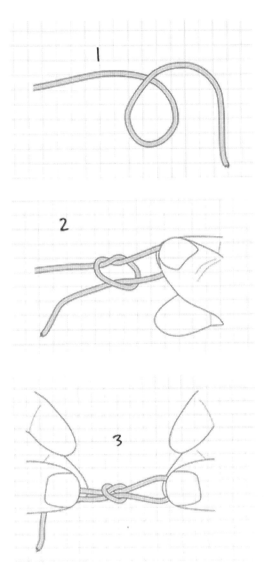

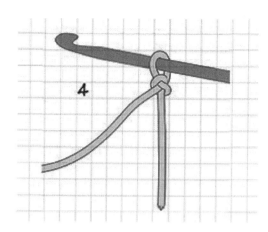

YARN OVER

To work a yarn over bring the yarn around the back of the hook and loop it over the top so that it catches in the hook.

CHAIN

With a loop on the hook, work a yarn over **(5)** and pull through the loop **(6)**.

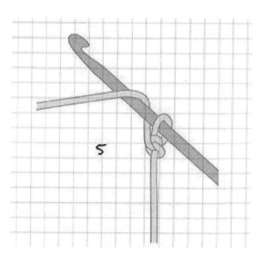

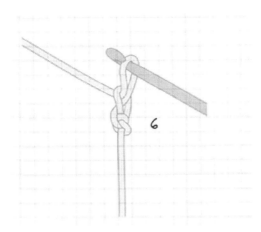

SLIP STITCH

Insert the hook into the work and make a yarn over. Pull through both the work and the loop on the hook **(7)**.

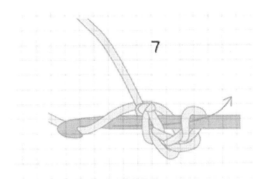

MAGIC RING

This is a way of starting a round if you don't want a visible hole at the centre of your work. It is quite an advanced bit of crochet magic but it is worth persisting with.

Make a loop with your fingers **(1)**, insert the crochet hook into the loop, yarn over and draw a loop through the centre of the ring **(2)**. Crochet stitches around the edge of the loop, working over both the loop and the tail end of yarn **(3)**, pull the tail end to tighten **(4)**, slip stitch to the first stitch to join.

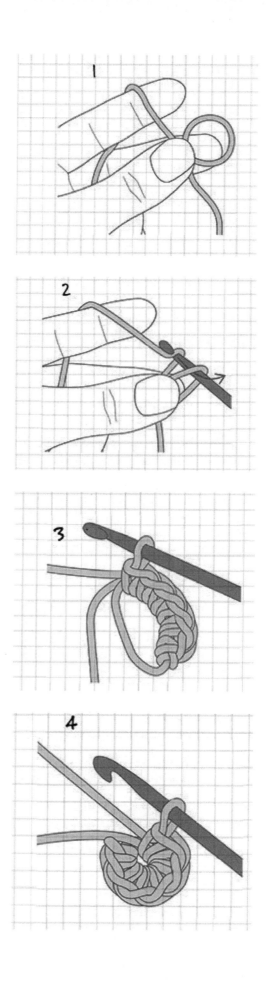

UK DOUBLE CROCHET
(US SINGLE CROCHET)

Insert the hook into the stitch, yarn over and draw a loop through so that you have 2 loops on the hook **(5)**, yarn over and pull through both loops **(6)** to create the finished stitch **(7)**. Continue working as many dc as required **(8)**.

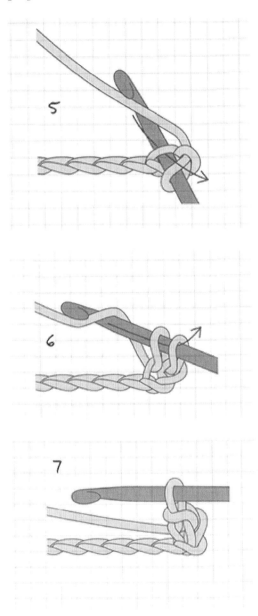

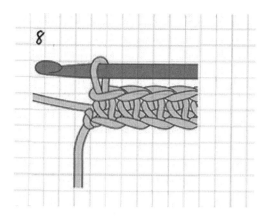

UK EXTENDED DOUBLE CROCHET
(US EXTENDED SINGLE CROCHET)

Insert the hook into the stitch, make a yarn over and draw a loop through so that you have 2 loops on the hook, yarn over and pull through one loop only **(9)**, yarn over and pull through both loops **(10)**.

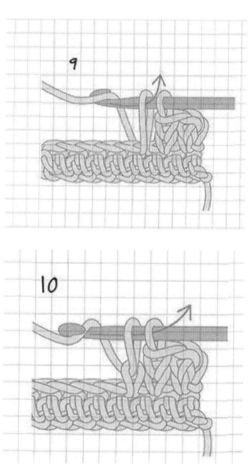

UK DOUBLE CROCHET INCREASE
(US SINGLE CROCHET INCREASE)

Work 2 uk double crochet (us single crochet) into the same stitch
(11).

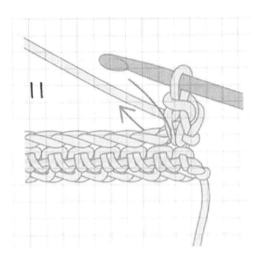

UK DOUBLE CROCHET 2 TOGETHER
(US SINGLE CROCHET 2 TOGETHER)

*Insert the hook into the stitch, make a yarn over and draw a loop
through so that you have 2 loops on the hook **(12)**, repeat from *
once, so that you have 3 loops on the hook **(13)**, yarn over and pull
through all 3 loops.

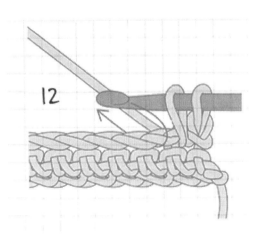

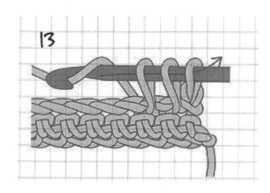

UK HALF TREBLE CROCHET
(US HALF DOUBLE CROCHET)

Yarn over hook and insert the hook into the stitch **(14)**, yarn over and draw a loop through so that you have 3 loops on hook **(15)**, yarn over and pull through all 3 loops.

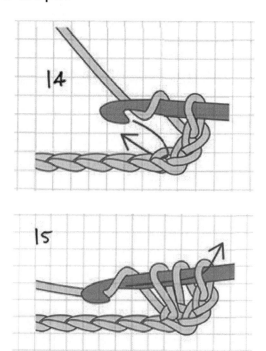

UK TREBLE CROCHET
(US DOUBLE CROCHET)

Yarn over hook and insert the hook into the stitch **(1)**, yarn over and draw a loop through so that you have 3 loops on the hook **(2)**, yarn over and pull through 2 loops **(3)**, yarn over and pull through remaining 2 loops **(4)**.

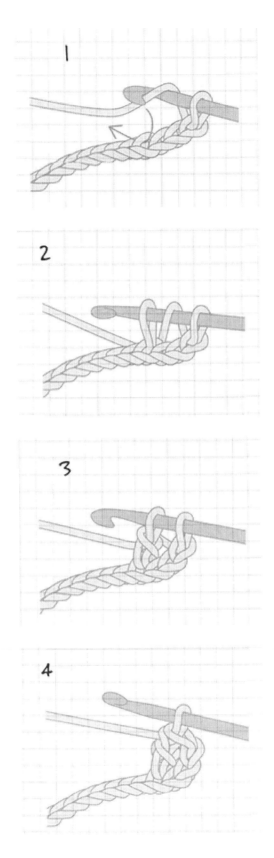

1

2

3

4

UK TREBLE CROCHET 2 TOGETHER
(US DOUBLE CROCHET 2 TOGETHER)

*Yarn over hook and insert the hook into the stitch, yarn over and draw a loop through so that you have 3 loops on the hook, yarn over and pull through 2 loops **(5)**, repeat from * once more, you will have 3 loops on the hook, yarn over and pull through all 3 loops **(6)**.

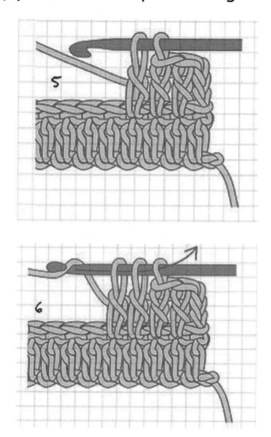

Sometimes, a tr2tog can be made into the same stitch or space.

UK TREBLE CROCHET 3 TOGETHER
(US DOUBLE CROCHET 3 TOGETHER)

*Yarn over hook and insert the hook into the stitch, yarn over and draw a loop through so that you have 3 loops on the hook, yarn over and pull through 2 loops, repeat from * twice more, you will have 4 loops on the hook, yarn over and pull through all 4 loops **(7)**.

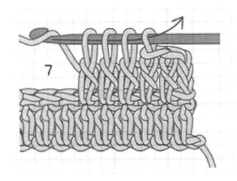

Sometimes, a tr3tog can be made into the same stitch or space.

HOW TO HAND SEW

SEWING STITCHES

WHIP STITCH

Whip stitch **(8)** is a hand sewing stitch traditionally used to join crochet or knitting. It is visible so will need to be in matching colours if you don't wish to see it or it can be worked in a contrasting colour as a design feature.

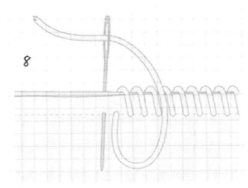

Line up the pieces you wish to stitch together, thread a yarn needle, secure the end with a knot and bring the needle from the back through to the front of both pieces. Take the needle over the top and through from the back to the front again. Keep going in this way to the end.

RUNNING STITCH

Thread the needle, insert the needle into the fabric from the back and pull out through the front **(9)**, insert the needle into the fabric a short distance further along from where it came out, from front to back, to make a stitch **(10)**. Continue in this way making evenly spaced stitches **(11)**.

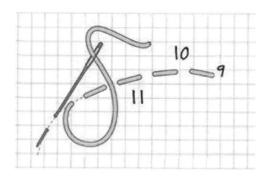

BACK STITCH

Thread the needle, insert the needle into the fabric from the back and pull out through the front **(12)**, insert the needle back into the fabric a short distance back from where you pulled it out to make a stitch **(13)**, insert the needle into the fabric from the back and pull out through the front a short distance further along from the end of the last stitch **(14)**, insert the needle back into the final hole of the last stitch. Continue by bringing the needle out a short distance from the end of the previous stitch and working back into it.

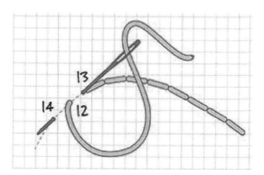

Printed in Great Britain
by Amazon

35313624R00128